# eBay Global the Smart Way

**Other Books by Joseph T. Sinclair**

eBay the Smart Way
eBay Business the Smart Way
eBay Motors the Smart Way

# eBay Global the Smart Way

### Buying and Selling Internationally
### on the World's #1 Auction Site

Joseph T. Sinclair

and

Ron Ubels

**American Management Association**
New York • Atlanta • Brussels • Chicago • Mexico City • San Francisco
Shanghai • Tokyo • Toronto • Washington, D.C.

382
Sin

Special discounts on bulk quantities of AMACOM books are available to corporations, professional associations, and other organizations. For details, contact Special Sales Department, AMACOM, a division of American Management Association, 1601 Broadway, New York, NY 10019.
Tel.: 212-903-8316. Fax: 212-903-8083.
Web site: www.amacombooks.org

This publication is designed to provide accurate and authoritative information in regard to the subject matter covered. It is sold with the understanding that the publisher is not engaged in rendering legal, accounting, or other professional service. If legal advice or other expert assistance is required, the services of a competent professional person should be sought.

Library of Congress Cataloging-in-Publication Data

Sinclair, Joseph T.
    eBay global the smart way : buying and selling internationally on the world's
    #1 auction site / Joseph T. Sinclair, Ron Ubels.
        p. cm.
    Includes bibliographical references and index.
    ISBN 0-8144-7241-9
    1. eBay (Firm) 2. Internet auctions. I. Ubels, Ron. II. Title.
    HF5478.S47372004
    382—dc22                                                    2004008416
                                                                CIP

Printing number
10   9   8   7   6   5   4   3   2   1

To my sisters Margaret Grace Sinclair Robb, Marilynn Dorothy Sinclair, and Suzanne Elizabeth Sinclair Williams.

Joseph T. Sinclair

To Gerry and Trudy Ubels, my dad and mom, for your example, strength of character, and faith. In memory of my brother Jeff. I miss you today and always.

Ron Ubels

# Contents

**Acknowledgments** ......................................................................**xiii**

**I. Introducing eBay Global** ....................................................**1**

    **1. Introduction** .............................................................**3**
        Pitfalls ............................................................................7
        Prototypes .....................................................................11
        eBay Basics ...................................................................11
        The Authors ..................................................................13
        Go for It! ......................................................................14
    **2. Global Prototypes** ..................................................**15**
        Prototypes .....................................................................16
        Non-Prototypes ............................................................21
        Summary .......................................................................22
    **3. Compliance, Finance, and Safety** .......................**23**

In Perspective ................................................. 24

Compliance ................................................... 25

Finance ......................................................... 26

Safety ............................................................ 26

Conclusion .................................................... 28

**4. Your Trade Reference System** .................. **29**

In Print ......................................................... 30

The Internet ................................................. 31

What Do You Need? ..................................... 33

Summary ....................................................... 35

**II. Customs** ....................................................... **37**

**5. Customs Clearance** ................................. **39**

Ports of Entry ............................................... 40

Value and Volume ......................................... 42

Paperwork ..................................................... 43

Summary ....................................................... 44

**6. Customs Documents** ............................... **45**

Unacceptable Consequences ......................... 46

The Documents ............................................. 46

Your Role ...................................................... 52

Physical Inspection ....................................... 54

Summary ....................................................... 54

**7. Import and Export Licenses** .................... **55**

Exporting ...................................................... 56

Importing ...................................................... 57

Quotas .......................................................... 57

Restricted Goods .......................................... 58

Licenses Abroad ........................................... 58

Summary ....................................................... 58

**8. Customs Brokers and Freight Forwarders** ........ **59**

Definitions .................................................... 60

Realities ........................................................ 61

Couriers ........................................................ 66

Post Offices ..................................................67
Customer Service ..........................................67
Summary ....................................................68

**9. Restricted Imports and Exports** ...................**69**
Restricted for Import .....................................70
Restricted for Export .....................................73
Rules and Regulations ...................................73
Plan Ahead ................................................74
Summary ....................................................74

**III. Finance** ...............................................**75**

**10. Taxes on Sales** .......................................**77**
Sales Tax ...................................................78
Value-Added Tax ..........................................80
Excise Tax ..................................................83
Complexity .................................................84
Summary ....................................................84

**11. Import Duties** ........................................**85**
Minimum Exemption .....................................86
Trade Treaty Exemption .................................86
Product Exemption .......................................87
Calculating the Duty .....................................87
Effect on Marketing ......................................91
Summary ....................................................92

**12. Means of Payment** ..................................**93**
Seller's Concerns ..........................................94
Buyer's Concerns ..........................................96
Types of Payment .........................................97
Beyond the Sales Price ..................................100
Summary ...................................................101

**13. Letters of Credit** ...................................**103**
Letter of Credit ...........................................104
Purpose ....................................................107
Paperwork .................................................107

Documentary Collection ............................................. 109
Coordination ........................................................ 109
Summary ............................................................. 110

**14. Currency Exchange** ............................................ **111**
Dealing with Fluctuations ........................................... 112
Exchanging Currency ................................................. 118
Currency Restrictions ............................................... 120
Summary ............................................................. 120

**15. Operational Costs** ........................................... **121**
Survey of Costs ..................................................... 122
Accounting .......................................................... 125
Summary ............................................................. 125

**16. Fraud** ....................................................... **127**
Follow the Rules .................................................... 128
Take Precautions .................................................... 130
Sellers Take Precautions ............................................ 131
Buyers Take Precautions ............................................. 133
Fraud Information Resources ......................................... 134

**IV. PayPal Finance** .............................................. **135**

**17. PayPal Basics** ............................................... **137**
How It Works ........................................................ 138
Verification ........................................................ 142
What and Where? ..................................................... 143
Summary ............................................................. 144

**18. Global Payments** ............................................. **145**
International Payments .............................................. 146
PayPal International ................................................ 149
Summary ............................................................. 152

**19. PayPal Import-Export** ........................................ **153**
Contingency Payments ................................................ 154
New Currency ........................................................ 158
Summary ............................................................. 158

**V. Shipping** ............................................................. **159**

   **20. Package Shipping** ............................................**161**
     Courier ........................................................162
     Post Office ...................................................168
     eBay Auction Ads .........................................170
     Packaging ....................................................170
     Summary .....................................................172

   **21. Bulk Shipping** .................................................**173**
     Containers ...................................................174
     Incoterms 2000 ...........................................176
     Summary .....................................................180

   **22. Insurance** .......................................................**181**
     Abroad .........................................................182
     Agreement ...................................................185
     Summary .....................................................185

**VI. Business and Culture** ..................................**187**

   **23. Communication** ..............................................**189**
     Email ............................................................190
     Telephone ....................................................192
     Language ......................................................198
     Summary .....................................................206

   **24. Business Culture and Travel Abroad** ...........**207**
     Why Travel? .................................................208
     Planning and Preparation ............................209
     Shopping .....................................................217
     Summary .....................................................218

   **25. Cross-Border Relationships** ..........................**219**
     Services ........................................................220
     Joint Ventures .............................................220
     Finding Joint Venturers ..............................223
     US Consulate ..............................................225
     Summary .....................................................226

**VII. Special Ventures** ................................................. **227**

   **26. Manufacturing Abroad** ................................. **229**
       How To? ...................................................230
       Template Products ......................................231
       Crafts ........................................................232
       VAT ..........................................................233
       At Home ....................................................233
       Summary ...................................................234

   **27. Warehousing** ............................................... **235**
       The Normal Way .........................................236
       The Smart Way ...........................................236
       Finding a Warehouse ..................................240
       Summary ...................................................241

   **28. Services and Digital Content** ...................... **243**
       Services ....................................................245
       Digital Content ...........................................248
       Summary ...................................................250

   **Appendix I  Top 10 Tips for Selling to Consumers Abroad** ............. **251**
   **Appendix II  Top 9 Tips for Buying on eBays Abroad** ...................... **253**
   **Appendix III  Top 8 Tips for Importing** ................................. **255**
   **Appendix IV  Top 7 Tips for Exporting** ................................. **257**
   **Appendix V  Foreign Countries** ..................................... **259**

   **Glossary** ......................................................... **281**

   **Bibliography** .................................................... **289**

   **Index** ............................................................. **293**

# *Acknowledgments*

To start, I would like to make a long overdue acknowledgement. Bob Chen has done a great job of creating book-jacket covers for the *eBay the Smart Way* series. The cover for this book is another in a series of great covers. Thanks Bob.

Edward Hinkelman, owner of World Trade Press and an author too, was nice enough to meet with me and provide me a copy of one of his many useful books. He's doing an impressive job of providing valuable information to the import-export industry, major corporations, and government agencies. Judy Vogele, a marine insurance account executive for ACE USA, Indemity Insurance of North America, and president of the Association of Marine Underiters of San Francisco, gave me a primer on transportation insurance, which helped add some authority to the brief chapter on insurance. Steve Gilman of Santori Trading, experienced in consumer import-export activities with India, was helpful too with background information on the import-export business. Thanks to all.

I would also like to acknowledge my co-author Ron Ubels who is an expert on import-export and one with special knowledge of eBay users' import and export activities. Without him the book would have been more academic and less practical. Thanks Ron.

Thanks also to the folks at AMACOM, including Jacqueline Flynn, Mike Sivilli, Kama Timbrell, and Andy Ambraziejus; and to my agent, Carole McClendon at Waterside Productions. A special thanks to my daughter Brook who put together Appendix V for me. Then too, I thank my wife Lani and son Tommy, for their patience and understanding during the long period it took to write this book.

Finally, I want to thank the eBay retailers who agreed to speak with me about their import-export activities on eBay. Clearly eBay is a hot bed of entrepreneurial activity that knows no bounds. Good luck to all.

Joseph T. Sinclair


To Sue, Nick, Tim and Lindsey. You inspire me to want to be the best I can be each day. You are life's greatest blessing.

Ron Ubels

# I

## *Introducing eBay Global*

# 1

# *Introduction*

What an exciting opportunity to expand your sales! Simply sell in other countries. Your potential market is bigger, and consequently profits can be greater. And American goods are very popular abroad. But before we get carried away with this idea, let's take a look at a major barrier, language. What is its significance? No one can argue that language doesn't matter.

Well, according to the Foreign Language Department of the Curso Experimental Bilingue, San Paulo, Brazil (*http://the_english_dept.tripod.com/esc.html*), English is used as a primary language by 375 million people, as a second language by another 375 million people, and as a foreign language by another 750 million people. That's a pretty big market. Potentially via eBay you can reach millions of consumers abroad—in English!

If, in addition, through eBay and other resources you can joint venture (partner) with people in other countries to increase your sales, selling internationally provides even greater opportunities. When you consider that English has become perhaps the primary language for commerce worldwide, you understand that by using English you can leverage your sales. That is, you can potentially sell well in markets that don't speak English by selling through a partner who does speak English.

It works the other way too. Consumers can find a wide variety of useful goods and exotic goods on eBay in 27 other countries for bargain prices. In addition, US importers through eBay and other resources can partner with people in other countries to import goods to sell in the US on eBay. Going global opens amazing opportunities. And what better way to go global than through eBay?

Today eBay operates auctions in the following countries (as of spring 2004):

Australia

Austria

Belgium

Canada

China (minority interest)

France

Germany

Hong Kong

Ireland

Italy

Mercado Libre (minority interest)

    Argentina

    Brazil

    Chile

    Columbia

    Ecuador

    Mexico

    Uruguay

    Venezuela

Netherlands

New Zealand

Singapore

South Korea

Spain

Sweden

Switzerland

Taiwan

United Kingdom

United States

eBay also owns PayPal, which is now established in 38 countries (as of spring 2004), which are listed in Chapter 18. PayPal enables you to conduct business in those countries more easily and more safely.

According to the 2003 eBay annual report, at the end of 2003 eBay had:

- 95 million registered users
- 41 million active users
- 40 million PayPal accounts
- A staggering 720 million page views per day!
- $85 million in sales each day!

About one-third of eBay is abroad. Extrapolating the end-of-year 2003 statistics, that means eBay had abroad:

- About 32 million registered members
- About 14 million active users
- As many as 13 million PayPal accounts

Does mean that you can increase your sales by 50 percent just by selling abroad? (If the US has two-thirds and countries abroad have one-third of the eBay volume, then reaching all of the eBay markets abroad from the US would theoretically increase your sales 50 percent.) Not likely. Many countries abroad have language barriers making significant market penetration without an English-speaking partner in those countries unlikely. Nonetheless, there is plenty of opportunity to expand your sales.

About 27 percent of goods exported via eBay go to Canada, 16 percent to Great Britain, 8 percent to Germany, and 6 percent to Japan. As you might expect, eBay business is a little more brisk in English-speaking countries.

Canada provides eBay US with 15,000 purchases per day. Over 25 percent of sales in 20 major subcategories are abroad. About 21 percent of the stamps, 18 percent of the music, 8 percent of the computers, and 5 percent of the auto parts are sold to buyers abroad. This gives you an idea of the range of sales abroad over a selection of major items.

Hey! If you have a global perspective, this eBay thing is really turning into something.

# Pitfalls

The pitfalls in carrying on commerce abroad are many. This is great news. Why? Because as every good businessperson knows, it excludes much of the competition. Those who take the trouble to learn the byways of foreign business will find greater opportunities than those who don't. Most often the rewards are greater than the extra effort. But let's survey some of the pitfalls.

## *Markets*

*eBay Business the Smart Way* said, "Oddly enough each item, no matter how similar to another item, has its own market. Don't assume that similar items will produce the same sales results." That is true in a national market. Add to that differences in affluence, culture, language, and business practices between countries and that observation is compounded. The pitfall is that you can't assume anything about an item's market until it is proven either by existing sales or by experimentation. Indeed, a common US item popular in France may have no significant sales in Brazil.

## *Paperwork*

Conducting business between countries is an exercise in paperwork. Bureaucracy controls the borders. Even for simple transactions, you must provide some paperwork. Moreover, the paperwork must meet the established bureaucratic standards, or the transaction may be jeopardized. Much of the agony caused by the required paperwork can be bypassed by the use of computer-generated documents, but you will

still have pay attention to detail. Or, you will have to pay to have someone else do it for you.

## Shipping

Other countries are often far away. That means shipping will be more
expensive for items sold in those countries than for local sales. This is
particularly true for overseas sales. Your choices aren't great. One to
eight days by air or one to eight weeks by ship. The latter is less expensive but not practical for consumer sales. Consequently, there will be
plenty of items that you can sell locally but not abroad. The cost of
shipping overseas will put many items out of the market.

## Payment

In the import-export business, businesspeople have traditionally used
cashier's checks, wire transfers, or letters of credit for payment. And
exchanges are often necessary from one currency into another. This
archaic infrastructure for payment is expensive. It nickels and dimes
you to death. A new less expensive infrastructure for payment is starting to be established, but it will take some time for it to become widespread. In the meanwhile, receiving payments and making payments
will continue to restrict the markets for many consumer goods.

## Communication

The computer age eliminates all long distance communications problems. Or, does it? Although email is instant and inexpensive, language
barriers still remain. You can't run a business depending on computer
translations. Consequently, where your potential customers don't
speak your language, your sales efforts may not be cost-effective.

## Taxes

Often duties must be paid for merchandise to cross borders. This is
simply a government tax on certain goods. This can become an important factor regarding whether you can make your sales profitable in a

foreign country. In addition, whether a duty is paid or not can depend on how an item is classified. Put in one class (category) the item is duty-free. Put in another category it has a 15 percent duty.

In addition, some countries have a sales tax or a value-added tax (VAT) or both. How those taxes are handled—or if they are even collected—can make or break a sales effort.

And to add insult to injury, every country is different when it comes to taxes.

## Third-Parties

Your goal in import-export is to take care of as much of the routine business and paperwork yourself as possible. If you have to get third-parties involved, it's going to cost money. Yet, it's often impossible to do what you need to do without third-party assistance. Accordingly, your profit margin must be higher for items sold abroad.

## Information

Anytime you must comply with government regulations, you need to know the regulations in order to comply. For instance, if you sell a dangerous item locally, you may have to comply with the different regulations of several different government agencies. This can be a nightmare, unless you can easily and cost-effectively access the information you need in order to comply. Thus, information becomes an important component of successfully making sales.

On an international scale, information is more often an important component of your sales effort because you have to comply with regulations in every country in which you do business. Many items, not just dangerous items, are subject to the regulations of each country. This means you will have to collect informational resources to use in your day-to-day business.

## Fraud

Fraud is rampant in many parts of the third world. Many underdeveloped countries cannot control massive fraud in the new online markets that the Internet has opened. This has caused a huge stumbling block in the path of increased global online commerce. Nonetheless, as businesspeople and consumers learn to discriminate between countries, the situation will improve greatly. Through PayPal and other safe payment mechanisms, many countries will come to dominate global online trade. Other countries may come to be shut out as their national reputations for fraud become widely acknowledged. The name of the import-export game is to learn which countries to trust, and already national reputations are beginning to emerge. The international markets are still huge even after you eliminate the countries that can't be trusted.

### Individuals

It's a little crazy to talk about trusting countries when it's really individuals who you can or cannot trust. In the most untrustworthy countries there will always be plenty of people you can trust. To be successful in business, however, you have to play the statistics. In countries where there are inadequate commercial regulations, controls, and law enforcement, the statistics work against you. It's not so crazy to be extra cautious when dealing with individuals from such countries.

Chapter 16 provides a list of the countries that already have a reputation for online fraud. Your best policy may be to refuse to do business with people from such countries. At the least, be super cautious about doing business with individuals from such countries.

## This Book

This book helps you get the information you need to carry on commerce safely and cost-effectively in foreign countries and avoid many of the pitfalls. As mentioned above, information is an important component of global commerce. You can't leave home without it and expect to do well. Therefore the goals of this book are to:

1. Explain key concepts of global commerce.

2. Explain certain important mechanisms necessary for doing business outside your own country.

3. Provide bountiful references (in English) to resources you can use for global commerce.

4. Help you make import-export via eBay safe and profitable.

Unfortunately, this book cannot feature a national-centric view of the global marketplace for each country. But many of the principles of international business are universal. The book uses the United States (US) and eBay in the US (eBay US) as well as Canada (CA) as the examples to illustrate how global online commerce works. Although some of the information herein is national-centric, we make an effort to express the concepts and mechanisms in more general terms so those readers outside the US and Canada will find the book useful.

# Prototypes

To make it easy to understand what information in this book is for you and what is for those who play a different role in international commerce than you, the book uses the prototypes outlined in Chapter 2. Keeping the prototypes in mind will help you understand the information in the chapters more easily.

# eBay Basics

This is a specialized eBay book. It doesn't cover the eBay basics. For the basics we recommend *eBay the Smart Way* Third Edition or a similar book. To learn the basics for operating a business on eBay we recommend *eBay Business the Smart Way* or a similar book. *eBay Global the Smart Way* assumes that you have used eBay and are confident in your basic eBay skills. If you don't yet have the necessary skills and confidence, you will probably not get the most out of this book. Moreover, this book assumes that you are confident that eBay is a safe place to buy and sell almost any type of goods, except in other countries. The purpose of this book is to provide you with the information you need to expand your eBay buying and selling to other countries with confidence and safety.

eBay is not a passing fad. It is the first great institutional marketplace of the new digital age. Indeed, it is the first great global online marketplace. It couldn't—and didn't—exist before the Internet. The Internet is here to stay, and the Internet is worldwide. And so is eBay. Consequently, it's to your benefit to learn the basics and develop the confidence to use eBay whether it's for your everyday buying and selling activities or for buying or selling as an eBay business.

And beyond that, it's also to your benefit to use eBay globally in order to maximize your buying and selling opportunities. This book will help you do so.

### Motors

If you're interested in buying and selling vehicles, try *eBay Motors the Smart Way*. However, we don't recommend casually buying or selling vehicles abroad on eBay. There are too many problems internationally, particularly when most vehicles are available in North America.

# The Authors

The authors don't have stock in eBay nor are they employed by eBay. We are free to tell it like it is, good or bad. eBay is a fabulous new international marketplace, but it has its shortcomings. It is particularly risky when buying in and selling in other countries via eBay—unless you have the knowledge to minimize the risk. We are excited and enthusiastic about eBay and in particular buying and selling globally. Nonetheless, we can be and are critical of eBay where appropriate. We present tactics, strategies, and good practices for making global trading via eBay as safe and as rewarding as using eBay at home.

The authors are Joseph T. Sinclair (Joe) and Ron Ubels (Ron). Joe has bought and sold casually via eBay globally. In addition, he has interviewed many full time eBay businesspeople who are active in global trading via eBay. He has practiced law, has been a commercial real estate broker and consultant, and has written books about Internet technology. He started writing his first book about eBay in 1998. This is his fourth book about the new eBay marketplace. His basic book *eBay the Smart Way* is now in its third edition.

Ron is a customs broker with 28 years experience in customs brokerage and international trade who works just south of Vancouver, Canada, on the Canadian side of the border with the US. He is a broker for A&A Contract Customs Brokers, Ltd. (*http://www.aacb.com*), a customs brokerage company that is active in handling eBay transactions and advising eBay businesses in regard to global trade as well as doing normal customs brokerage. Ron has given lectures to eBay sellers in Vancouver and Victoria, British Columbia.

He has worked in various management capacities in the industry in both operations and sales. He has extensive experience working with US and Canadian companies in developing export markets and has also devoted time over the past eight years to public speaking in the US, speaking on international trade and marketing issues. He has worked extensively in partnership with a number of international transportation and courier companies as well as government and state support agencies.

Ron is a past President of the British Columbia Division of the Canadian Society of Customs Brokers and has also served on the Society's national Board of Directors.

# Go for It!

If you're reading this book, you're probably a seasoned eBay participant. You have been making history. You've turned a small online collectibles marketplace into a huge general online marketplace, an institutional marketplace such as the New York Stock Exchange. That's acknowledged today. What isn't acknowledged yet but is happening right now is that eBay is turning into a safe and rewarding global marketplace. In just a few years, the world will wake up to the fact that eBay has become a significant force in international commerce. In other words, you're making history again.

If you think you got into eBay late and missed the ground floor, expanding your sales abroad gives you the opportunity to get in on the ground floor of the latest eBay expansion. If you're an old eBay business looking for new ways to make more sales, exporting via eBay opens new markets for you. If you've already tested the faraway markets, additional information can help you resolve problems and perhaps expand sales even further. If you just want to do some exotic shopping abroad without leaving your desk, eBays abroad offer amazing opportunities. Or, if you sell on eBay, sooner rather than later you will have a winning bidder from abroad. How will you handle the sale?

This book will help you use eBay globally the smart way.

# 2

# *Global Prototypes*

The byways of global trade are complex enough without confusing readers as to who we are talking to in this book. With that in mind, in this chapter we have established some prototype readers. If you find that you don't fit into one of these prototypes, this book may not be for you. Through these prototypes, we attempt to keep all the topics relevant to a broad range of eBay users while at the same time making it clear that this book was not written for large businesses that can staff a substantial import-export department.

# Prototypes

Read the prototypes and determine where you fit in. Many of the chapters or chapter sections in this book focus on one prototype or another. Look for chapters or sections that apply the topic of the chapter to your particular activities on eBay.

## eBay Consumer

There are individuals who buy and sell on eBay for their own consumption or to rid themselves of unwanted assets. Consumers in the US are featured throughout this book. Nonetheless, it is easy for eBay consumers in other countries to identify with consumers in the US and get a lot out of this book too.

### Consumer Buyers

You can buy on eBays abroad. It's quite easy at English language eBays such as the United Kingdom (Great Britian or GB) ) and Australia (AU). It's more difficult at eBay France or eBay Italy, but not as difficult as you might think. You will be surprised at how well Babel Fish and other software language translators work for consumers (see Chapter 23). Although it's true that:

Shipping is likely to be more expensive;

You might have to pay a huge value-added tax (VAT) in the other country; and

For expensive items you may have to pay the customs duty.

Still, you can buy exotic things that aren't available in the US and Canada or are only available at wildly inflated prices. This is an exciting opportunity for consumers. Give it a try.

### Consumer Sellers

Almost everyone who sells sooner or later has inquiries or bids from buyers abroad. Do you want to eliminate such consumers from the market for your items? That's not a good idea. Ultimately, it means less money in your pocket. You need to be ready to sell to people abroad and be set up to receive secure payment.

# eBay Retail Business

These are small businesses in the US and Canada that buy and sell on eBay US to make money. Such businesses do most of their business via eBay. These businesses might be individuals, Mom & Pop (husband & wife) businesses, or businesses with few employees or even no employees. Or, they might even be larger businesses with as many as a dozen employees.

These businesses export items one item at a time to consumers abroad. They import items one at a time, or at most, in small quantities.

## Retail Sellers

The eBay business that fits this profile is one that sells to consumers abroad, one item at a time or perhaps several items at a time.

The demand from abroad via eBay can increase your markct by 30 percent, 60 percent, 90 percent, who knows? It will be different for every product you sell. What's certain is that generally there's plenty of demand from abroad. What's also certain is that many eBay sellers have been enjoying this extra demand for a long time and have profited from the increased sales. Don't sell yourself short—literally. Expand your markets by getting set up to handle orders from other countries. Yes, there are problems, but that's what this book is for—to make selling abroad more secure.

Again, remind yourself that there are 1.5 billion English-speaking people in the world, and only about 300 million of them are in North America.

Example: One eBay retailer (one person) buys hard disks (for computers) from IBM in bulk in the US, where they are inexpensive. He resells them individually on eBays abroad, primarily in English-speaking countries where they are expensive. His biggest market is Australia.

### Retail Buyers

A retail buyer that fits this profile is one that may acquire items on eBays abroad to sell at home on eBay US. As *eBay Business the Smart Way* points out, the most difficult task for an eBay business is finding inventory to sell at a profit. eBays abroad are great places to find exotic items to sell in the US at a good markup.

Another retail buyer that fits this profile is one that buys items in small quantities abroad (not on eBay) and imports the items via a courier service (e.g., FedEx). To do this, you have to develop sources of inventory any way you can. Dealing with retail sellers on eBays abroad is one way to develop sources of inventory.

Note that a retail buyer can act like a consumer to find potential items for inventory. Just go shopping on a few of the eBays abroad. It's a great way to get ideas, make contact with volume sellers, and otherwise get your import activities off the ground.

## eBay Import-Export Business

These are small businesses in the US that actually import or export goods in bulk and generally use surface shipping rather than courier shipping. This business takes more capital than the normal eBay retail business, and businesses that fit this profile tend to be a little bigger than eBay retail businesses.

### Importers

The eBay businesses that match this profile import goods in bulk to warehouses (garages, mini storage units) in the US or Canada and then sell the items on eBay US to consumers. Let's face it. Americans consume a huge amount of products from abroad. (The trade deficit is currently out of control.) Tens of thousands of businesses abroad want to export to the US and Canada. If you have the capital to purchase in bulk, you can find many sources of profitable inventory in other countries. Many of these goods are identical to or similar to ones we already use every day (e.g., small appliances and other mass produced goods).

What's the sweet spot of this corner of eBay business? Foreign closeouts! If you can find a closeout offered by a company abroad and import it, you can realize profits you never expected from an eBay business.

Example: One eBay retailer in the Midwest had three bicycle shops and 70 employees. He closed the shops. Now with only 11 employees he retails large quantities of bicycles and other sports equipment on eBay. He buys foreign and imports closeouts such as 800 bicycles from Italy and 3,000 sports heart monitors from Taiwan. He sells them individually on eBay US.

## Exporters

The eBay business that fits this profile has two potential markets, eBay US and eBays abroad. This eBay business exports goods in bulk to another country to be stored in a warehouse or a cross-border warehouse (see Chapter 27). It then sells the items one at a time on eBay US to consumers in that country.

This business uses the warehouse to create efficiencies and improve customer service in a country where it has many eBay customers. It uses the warehouse for drop shipping, in effect. The shipping cost is less for the buyer, and presumably the shipping time is reduced too. Moreover, the warehousing can make the selling operation more efficient.

Another use of exporting might be to store inventory for sales resulting from auctioning items on an eBay abroad. For instance, warehousing inventory in England (GB) to sell on eBay UK may make sense. After all, it's a large English-speaking market.

eBay exporters sometimes have a partner or agent in the other country where they do business. For instance, an eBay exporter might have a partner (joint venturer) or a relationship with a warehouse company, freight forwarder (shipping agent), or a customs broker in order to process the goods routinely in the other country. Moreover, it's almost essential to have a partner to sell in volume on an eBay abroad in a non-English-speaking country. It's usually the partner's job to do the warehousing, marketing, advertising, and eBay sales.

## Foreign eBay Business

This prototype is the equivalent of an eBay business but one that operates in another country. It is easy for eBay businesses in other countries to identify with eBay businesses in the US. Every country needs to import and export goods, and small businesses do a good job of it.

## Traditional Import-Export Business

These are small businesses in the import-export business in the US that may not do any buying or selling on eBay. Most of the information relevant to these businesses is in Chapters 17, 18, and 19 on PayPal. eBay bought PayPal in late 2002 when PayPal wasn't limited to just eBay users or eBay transactions. PayPal continues to be available to everyone and provides services convenient for small import-export businesses that don't buy or sell on eBay.

Note that PayPal is an exciting new service for global payment that's available to any business. That's why the PayPal chapters include a non-eBay prototype.

### How Small?

How small is small when it comes to import-export businesses? Well, small businesses that have found a profitable niche have always done well in the import-export business. Today, banks are pushing credit cards with high credit limits. For example, a $50,000 credit limit is not uncommon. Suppliers are accepting credit card payments. Consequently, an individual with a $50,000 credit-limit credit card (or five $10,000 credit-limit credit cards) can go into the import-export business. Indeed, in some cases if you can execute your buying and selling activities quickly with precise timing, you may be able to use credit cards and completely avoid paying interest or other credit charges.

A small import-export business of this type is not a good candidate to *enjoy* working with a bank—and paying bank fees—in order to make payments in other countries. If there is a less expensive and less bureaucratic way of making payments, the traditional import-export business will find it. And PayPal is a potential solution, enabling small import-export businesses to avoid banks.

# Non-Prototypes

Because this is an eBay book, it doesn't make sense to tailor this book for certain people. If you just started working in the import-export department of a corporate business, say a manufacturer with 600 employees, you may find that this book does not provide the information you need to do your job well, even if your business sells on eBay. This book is primarily intended for individuals buying and selling and for small businesses that cannot afford to staff a substantial import-export department.

The book is not for:

Large businesses, usually incorporated, with dozens or hundreds of employees. Such businesses that have a considerable volume of imports or exports operate cost-effectively in ways that would put a significant financial burden on smaller businesses. These large businesses usually do only a small percentage of their business, if any, on eBay.

Large corporate businesses that operate with a scope and breath well beyond the coverage of this book. They usually do only a very small percentage of their business via eBay. Such corporations as General Electric and Kraft Foods are examples.

Consequently, in the chapters ahead we have fashioned this book for the prototypes that pertain to either consumers or small businesses. If you don't fit into one of these categories, we recommend you read a traditional book on import-export.

### The Basics

Even if you work for a large enterprise, reading this book is not a total misadventure. Anyone reading this book ought to come away with a basic knowledge of the import-export business. In addition, the resources this book puts at your fingertips will save you countless hours of finding such resources on your own.

## Summary

This book can't be all things to all people. By limiting this 300-page book to eBay consumers, small eBay retail businesses, small eBay import-export businesses, and small foreign eBay retailers, we are still providing coverage that is less robust than we would like to present. To extend coverage to larger businesses, even though they may sell on eBay, would be stretching the coverage too thin. Thus, we focus on the small business world that typifies eBay. Nonetheless, anyone reading this book will come away with sound basics for the import-export business.

# 3

# Compliance, Finance, and Safety

You have to deal with three important issues when you start selling abroad or import products from abroad. The first is compliance. You need to meet governmental regulations, not only the ones of your own government but those of governments abroad too. Those government regulations are such things as valuation, origin, trade quotas, import-export licenses, hazardous substance controls, and the like. Sometimes it isn't easy to do business across national borders. But even when it is easy, it's still likely to be a dance with the bureaucracy.

Compliance is becoming a much bigger issue than it has been in the past. Governments are striving for simplification and efficiency at the border. But they are doing so in order to focus more on compliance. For instance, Canada in 2002 introduced the Administrative Monetary Penalty System (AMPS), which allows goods to pass through customs easily and quickly but audits the paperwork later. If the paperwork is out of compliance, monetary penalties are accessed.

You have to conduct your financial affairs across national borders as well. That tends to be more complicated than doing business in-country, even for simple cash purchase transactions. Indeed, import-export banking goes all the way back to the very beginning of modern banking in mid-second-millennium Europe. It takes a fair amount of bureaucratic attention. Then too, there are often governmental restrictions on payments.

Finally, there's the issue of safety. Concerns for safety go hand in hand with financial arrangements. Sellers like to get paid safely. That is, a seller wants to make sure he gets paid by a buyer far away in a foreign country. Likewise, a buyer wants to make sure he receives the goods for which he paid someone far away in a foreign country. These assurances to both buyers and sellers require bureaucratic byways normally not present in a domestic transaction.

Safety is a transportation issue also. Overseas air freight risks of loss, theft, or damage are perhaps much the same as domestic air freight, but surface shipment takes much longer and often poses greater risks.

# In Perspective

This chapter provides you a dose of reality in regard to extending your retail business beyond your national borders. But don't let the reality smother you. You can increase your sales just by being willing to sell your products abroad and doing so. You can increase your sales even more by creating a strategy and sales program to sell abroad. Such sales, however, come at a cost. It is more difficult to sell abroad than domestically.

There are two points to remember as you read this chapter. First, if you get organized to handle the extra bureaucratic effort it takes to sell abroad, it will become much easier. Digital automation can be helpful in this regard. Second, the greater effort and risks that it takes to sell abroad will keep many of your competitors out of the overseas markets. These two factors make selling abroad a great opportunity for you to increase your sales.

# Compliance

Compliance is as easy as sending additional documents with your products when you ship, or as difficult (expensive) as hiring a freight forwarder or customs broker to move your products across national borders. It depends on the scope of your imports or exports. Below is a list of general factors. Not all are present in every transaction.

- Paying or requesting refunds for value added tax
- Paying duties
- Complying with import quotas and restrictions
- Complying with foreign product regulations (e.g., health)
- Providing proper documentation
- Obtaining required import or export licenses, if applicable

For instance, if you sell one item on eBay to a buyer abroad, just enclosing a customs invoice that meets import requirements may be all you need to do. You can easily handle this just by being well organized. If you want to export 200 items to France to be sold on eBay France by your joint venturer there, however, you might need to hire a customers broker, get a US export license, get a French import license, and comply with additional bureaucratic requirements.

# Finance

Even a cash payment often becomes a more bureaucratic transaction when you make payment abroad. Your cashier's check (foreign draft) has to be a credible check; it has to go through a foreign banking system; and there will probably be an exchange from your currency into the currency of the buyer's country. Then too, you are more likely to use a wire transfer when making a payment abroad, and that means making arrangements.

For bulk purchases, instant payments are not necessarily the norm, and contingent payments (payments based on a certain requirement being met) are common. A letter of credit, a common type of contingent payment for imports and exports, requires bank administration both for your bank in the US and the other party's bank abroad. Even the most simple letter of credit is more complex than a check.

Thus, finance is not necessarily something that comes as naturally as it does when operating domestically. It requires prior arrangements to be made.

# Safety

Finance is a risk domestically. It's difficult to sell at retail without buying inventory on credit or to sell in bulk without accepting credit. It's difficult for consumers to buy energetically without credit. Thus, the risks that accompany credit are normally part of the retailing landscape, even on eBay.

The risk of fraud is likewise present, too, and fraud is not a one-way street. There is buyers' fraud and sellers' fraud. The criminals work the system both ways.

What's the remedy in the US? Well, you probably aren't going to get your money back in a case of nonpayment or fraud if the stakes are low. The legal costs of a civil suit or the likelihood of a successful criminal action will probably prevent you from getting any satisfaction.

Nonetheless, you can make the life of the offending party miserable. You can file a bad credit report on a creditor who doesn't pay. You can file complaints with the Federal Trade Commission, the FBI, the Postal Inspector, or a state attorney general in a fraud case.

If the stakes are high, it might be worth your time and resources in the US to start a civil suit; or, it might worth it to ask a district attorney to pursue a criminal action in a case of fraud.

The bottom line is that your chances of collecting what you've got coming are not very good in the US. Nevertheless, there are potential consequences for anyone who doesn't pay their bills or who commits fraud. This keeps our domestic commerce system a reasonably safe place to do business.

So what's the point? The point is that there are, in effect, no such consequences abroad. To bring a civil suit abroad has potential complexities and expenses that would only make it cost-effective for claims well beyond the scope of the volume of business for which this book has been written. Likewise, to bring a criminal complaint and get a foreign government to successfully pursue it would entail an effort that few would be willing to undergo. Without consequences, the credit risks and risk of fraud are likely to be much higher, and indeed they are.

With a minimum of precautions, you can sell without great risk in the US. You have to take great precautions to sell abroad, or the risk you will take will likely be unbearable. And that's what safety is all about.

There is another type of safety that puts you at risk financially too. That's the risk that something will happen to the goods en route, the risk of loss or theft. We worry a lot about loss or theft in transportation in the US, usually enough to get insurance on the shipment of expensive items. On shipments abroad the risk is greater, and insurance is, practically speaking, mandatory.

What are the additional transportation risks?

- Longer distances

- Longer travel times (particularly for surface shipping)

- Handling that may not be as tightly controlled in some places abroad as in the US

- Multiple carriers handling the shipment

- Potential customs problems

Consequently, even with a carrier such as UPS, you may find shipments abroad more risky than domestic shipments.

# Conclusion

Yes, doing business on eBay abroad is not the same as doing business at home. It's more complex and requires extra effort. But it's like anything else. Practice makes perfect. With a little practice, you should have no trouble dealing with the compliance, finance, and safety issues.

# 4

## *Your Trade Reference System*

So many countries, so many regulations. And then too, your own government has a labyrinth of regulations you must meet. You have to face it, but you also have to make it easy on yourself. What can you do?

You need to do what you do already as an eBay seller, only on a grander scale. You need to build up a system of information to which you can refer to get answers. Let's call it a *trade reference system*.

For instance, look at shipping in the US, which every eBay seller must do. You must know where to go to get quotes on shipping costs to inform prospective buyers. Indeed, you must know where to get the least expensive shipping. That's part of the buyer's cost of buying; and the less expensive the shipping, the more items you can sell. Does that mean you have to keep printed UPS, USPS, and FedEx rate schedules at your warehouse (or garage)? Does that mean you have to know where to go on the Web to get such rate schedules? Whatever it means, you have to have easy access to the information somehow to get the job done.

Now, to shipping requirements and pricing you add information on customs, duties, trade quotas, restricted commerce, exchange rates, and a myriad of other import-export information, and you start to get the picture. You need to have large volumes of information at your fingertips, whether online or offline, to buy or sell in countries abroad.

Because everyone will have a different situation in regard to what (and how) they either import or export, no one trade reference system fits all. You need to build your own.

# In Print

There are dozens of publications (out of hundreds) you might want to include in your office. It's a matter of convenience. If you can find the publications you need in your local library and don't need them often, going to the library is a workable solution for you. If you have a local Export Assistance Center or Port of Entry at which you can look at publications and you don't need them often, that might be a workable solution. A university business school library nearby might have what you need too. Most business people put a premium on their time, however, and the convenience of having the information in-house is often worth the cost. Take a look at the book list at World Trade Press, Novato, California (*http://worldtradepress.com*). They have some books you may want to acquire for your trade reference system.

Any printed publications you use, either inside your office or outside, are a part of your trade reference system. Keep in mind that once you start accumulating publications, you might want to keep a list (index) of what you have. Why not use a card catalog? That's what libraries do. You can do the same with index cards. Of course, libraries have now put their card catalogs online (electronic list). And it should be easy for you to create an online list using a word processor.

Is this idea important for small offices? Yes. It's always important for business efficiency to keep organized. Having the publications (and forms) you need at your fingertips is essential for the import-export business, where in many situations you need substantial information to do business. Is this idea important for larger offices? Yes, with the addition of another idea. The publications should have a special location where personnel can always find them—a mini library.

# The Internet

The Internet, of course, is not only a great resource but a cost-effective one. Use the Web as a prime resource for your trade reference system.

## *Websites*

Most of us have come to rely on the Web as a major source of information for business as well as for personal use. Fortunately, there is no shortage of trade information on the Web. For buying and selling abroad, you will want to build your own online reference center in your browser bookmarks. (Note that Microsoft calls bookmarks by the name "favorites.")

In the bookmarks (favorites) section of your browser, you can create folders. Create a folder named *Trade*, and put all your bookmarked links into the Trade folder. That way, all the links you need for import-export resources will be in one place, easy to find.

Note that you can also create subfolders under your Trade folders to further organize your import-export resources.

There are many dozens of complete websites and other resources on the Web related to or specifically dedicated to the import-export industry. With a little effort, you won't have any trouble finding what you need and bookmarking it for future use.

Good sources of online information, particularly for exporting to consumers, are the couriers: UPS, FedEx, and others.

## *Portals*

Isn't there just one Web portal where one can go to get almost everything one needs? In fact, there is. World Trade Press, the company that publishes so many import-export books, operates an import-export portal called World Trade Reference (*http://worldtraderef.com*). Many import-export banks and companies buy site licenses (a one-fee license to use the portal that covers all their employees). Although a subscription is comparatively expensive for a single subscriber, the information is constantly updated and is always at your fingertips. The World Trade Reference portal includes the following:

- Glossaries and dictionaries
- Some World Trade Press books (electronic versions)
- US Forms and documents (PDFs)
- Forms and documents for 50 countries (PDFs)
- Resources for importing into the US
- Resources for international trade
- Trade terms (over 3,000) in eight languages
- Country data
- Measurement converters

- Global time clock

- Searchable database of 86,000 US Customs rulings

It contains much more, but the list above will whet your appetite. You can get a free 3-day trial subscription at the website.

### Build Your Own Private Portal

Don't want to pay a subscription fee for access to information? Much of the information available on the World Trade Reference is also available free in different forms and formats elsewhere on the Web. If you spend the time and effort to put together a trade reference system, you can save the subscription fee.

Many of the customs brokers and freight forwarders operate information-laden websites that are like portals where you can find a lot of information. For instance, try the website operated by Ron's company, A&A Contract Customs Brokers, *http://aacb.com*.

# What Do You Need?

What information you need is specifically related to your business. For instance, if you import clothes to sell on eBay, if will have to pay attention to textile quotas. That requires a lot of information. Importing most other merchandise requires less information.

## Consumer Sales

"OK," you say to yourself, "I just want to sell a few trinkets to consumers abroad. Do I really need a trade reference system?" Well, that depends. Let's say you sell an item that consumers from Belgium, France, and Romania, but nowhere else, regularly order. It doesn't take an extensive trade reference system to support such sales. But that's not the normal case. More typical would be orders from random countries across the globe. It's a global economy, American products are popular, and a guy in Singapore is just as likely to bid on your eBay auction as a gal in St. Louis. You need to be ready to ship to over 200 countries.

Therein lies the rub, as they say. It's not that the import-export business is necessarily complicated. Just exporting consumer products one at a time isn't complex. Rather, it's that there are so many countries to keep track of, each with its own regulations. Keep in mind, you don't have to *know* the information you use. You just have to be able to look it up quickly and easily. Or, for exporting consumer products, you just have to know what forms to use. It's this extra wrinkle of selling to consumers abroad that makes the difference in the amount of information you use to make a consumer sale. And with over 200 different countries, there are going to be different ways of doing things.

What has been said here so far assumes a passive view of sales abroad. If you want to be proactive, that is, if you want to encourage sales, you will need even more information about each country, its consumers, and its regulations.

## Bulk Imports and Exports

Clearly, when you import or export in bulk, the amount of information you need to operate a successful eBay import-export business is much greater than just selling to consumers abroad. This is particularly true when you deal in restricted goods such as clothing, agricultural products, and the like for which quotas, public health, safety, or other considerations apply. A trade reference system is crucial.

To a certain extent you can rely, if you choose, on customs brokers or freight forwarders to do much of the administrative work for you. But that comes at a price. And, in any event, you still have to provide the overall management of the process. Thus, import-export information is still important to your success.

# Summary

A trade reference system is simply the idea that you will need an extra measure of information to do business abroad, and you need to acquire the information, organize it, and make it easy and convenient to use. There is no one system that fits all. There is no one product that you can buy. Building a trade reference system is a project—your project.

One final note. This book gives you a good start on building your trade reference system. It sure took us a long time to put together all the resources this book includes.

# II

## Customs

*5*

# *Customs Clearance*

Customs has traditionally existed to collect duties (tariffs) on goods being imported. It has another historical purpose too. It restricts the flow of certain goods that the government wants to restrict, for whatever reasons. In more recent history, customs also restricts the flow of goods for public health or public welfare reasons. For instance, agricultural produce must comply with US Department of Agriculture regulations set up to ensure a safe food supply. In fact, for many products, you may have to get the approval of a specific government agency before you can clear customs. The focus has shifted from revenue to protection.

### eBay Goods

Most products aren't restricted, and most of the products sold on eBay are not likely to be restricted. Clothing and electronics are exceptions.

In this era of terrorist threats, it would be nice to think that all goods coming into the country are inspected. That would be impossible, however, without greatly increasing the ranks of customs inspectors. Rather, custom clearance relies on paperwork. If your paperwork is in order, your products are likely to move easily through customs (see Chapter 6). If not, a customs broker may have to expend extra effort to get your product through customs, thus potentially incurring an additional expense.

### Inspecting Goods

Customs everywhere is stepping up inspections as terrorism threatens. Although customs can't inspect everything, that doesn't necessarily mean that you will avoid inspections.

# Ports of Entry

Products that enter the US must go through customs. The question is, where? The answer is, ports of entry. At each port of entry, there is a customs office. In the good old days, the ports of entry were on the East Coast, Gulf Coast, and West Coast. The St. Lawrence Seaway (*http://www.greatlakes-seaway.com/en/seawaymap/index.html*) opened the Great Lakes states to ocean-going shipping, and those states became, in effect, another coast (see Figure 5.1). Today with air freight, a port of entry can be almost anywhere there's a jetport (airport that handles commercial jet traffic). Almost every state has one or more ports of entry.

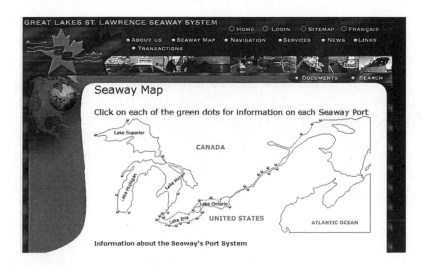

**Figure 5.1    Great Lakes St. Lawrence Seaway System.**

Keep in mind, however, what logic dictates. If you live in Utah and have something shipped via surface transport from Taiwan, you will have to clear it through customs in the ocean port in which it arrives (e.g., Seattle). You can't clear it through the port of entry in Salt Lake City, Utah. That port of entry is for products coming into Salt Lake City by air (see *http://www.econdev.slco.org/content/trans_p1.cfm*).

Keep in mind, too, the obvious. The points along national borders through which people and goods travel (i.e., on roads) are also ports of entry. The cities of El Paso on the US side and Juarez across the Rio Grande River in Mexico are examples.

## *Lists*

The US Ports of Entry supervised by the US Customs offices are important because all goods coming into the US must go through them. When you import something, you will naturally want the goods to arrive at the nearest port of entry to your warehouse—if you have control of the delivery point. You can get complete details on each port of entry office at the US Customs & Border Protection website (*http://www.customs.gov/xp/cgov/toolbox/contacts/ports/*).

For Canada go to *http://www.cbsa-asfc.gc.ca/E/pub/cm/d1-1-1/pdf/d1-1-1b-e.pdf* to get a list of the many Canadian ports of entry.

# Value and Volume

The amount of paperwork and effort required to clear customs varies with value, volume, and type of goods.

## Duty-Free Maximums

If you import products into the US under $200 US in value in a shipment, one shipment at a time, they will likely move through customs without problems (and without a customs broker) so long as the paperwork is correct. In Canada, the maximum is $20 CA. Of course, if a product falls into a restricted category, it may be necessary to take additional steps to clear it through customs.

Why do governments make such exception? It's simply to lighten the work load for customs officers at ports of entry.

## Bulk Shipments

If you import products in bulk, it becomes more complex. In the US, for a shipment in excess of $2,000 US a formal clearance is required, and you will have to have a customs broker handle the clearance for you. The Canadian threshold is $1,600 CA. This may seem farfetched for a small eBay business, but we know eBay businesses that import thousands of items at a time to ultimately sell on eBay US several at a time.

## *In Between*

What about shipments coming into the US in between $200 US and $2,000 US? Or, shipments coming into Canada in between $20 CA and $1,600 CA? They don't require formal clearance. It should be easy to clear them through customs, but you still have to pay duty and will need a customs broker.

Customs brokers are needed to ensure compliance. The customs brokers are at the port of entry, and the buyer-importer may be hundreds of miles away. The mode of transportation is a factor too. The buyer may live in an inland airport city with a port of entry, but the goods arrive by ship in a coastal city.

# Paperwork

Paperwork is a tough notion. The seller (exporter) prepares the documents. But the documents usually don't mean much to the exporting country. The documents mean everything to the buyer (importer), because the buyer has to clear customs in the country of importation. If the paperwork is not perfect, a product is quite likely to be stopped by customs. That means that a customs broker must expend extra effort with customs to get a product through.

### *Customs Broker*

If you work on clearing a product through customs yourself, it will take time and effort. If you do it often enough, you will become an expert, and your efforts may become justified. Most eBay businesses, however, will opt to hire a customs broker to clear a product through customs.

The problem here is that the party with the least incentive to do a good job with the paperwork is the party who does the paperwork, the seller (exporter). Nonetheless, the seller does have some motivation to do the paperwork carefully. First, there's customer service. If one doesn't provide good customer service—if one doesn't do the paperwork well—one isn't likely to stay in business. The poor paperwork will cause compliance problems for the buyer. Second, there's professional pride. Most people like to do a job well, and professional export-import businesspeople (or professional eBay businesspeople) presumably want to provide professionally done paperwork. Third, it may be part of the requirements of a contingent payment that the seller provide competent documentation (i.e., paperwork that works). See Chapter 13.

That's all well and good, but the above analysis may not fit all eBay transactions. If eBay buyers and sellers buy or sell abroad only occasionally, they will be prone to mistakes out of inexperience or from inattention where careful attention to detail is due. The trouble is that the penalty falls on the buyer-importer. When the paperwork is not adequate for customs, the buyer may incur a higher fee with a customs broker.

You can research the paperwork needed for each country at the various customs websites linked to the World Customs Organization (WCO) website at *http://www.wcoomd.org*.

## Summary

Customs clearance is the starting point for understanding the import-export business. The more you learn about customs both for the US, Canada, and other countries, the more confidence you will have in doing business abroad. Customs is a potential bottleneck that may inhibit your import-export activities. It is also a bottleneck that may inhibit your thinking. That is, it may scare you out of importing or exporting. Once you learn about it, however, you can handle it. You can overcome the bottleneck in your mind and successfully clear your products through customs even if it just means learning how to hire a customs broker.

# 6

## *Customs Documents*

If you're a seller and you learn only one thing from this book, that should be: to provide complete and accurate custom documents. Customs floats on a sea of paperwork. Think about it. If customs officials inspected every product crossing borders, customs officials would become as numerous as fast food workers. Instead they handle paperwork, and in that paperwork they look for complete, accurate, and understandable information. They look for compliance. If you do not provide that information, the consequences are unacceptable.

# Unacceptable Consequences

The unacceptable consequences fall potentially first on you and then on your customers. With incomplete or confusing documentation, the carrier may just return the item to you. Now you're in a bind because the buyer is waiting for the package, and you have to handle and ship the package a second time—not an efficient way to do business.

But worse, what if the package gets to customs, and customs stops it? Now, your buyer's customs broker has to try to clear it with faulty documentation, even though the merchandise may be under the duty-free maximum. The vast majority of buyers are not in a situation where it's practical to clear an item through customs themselves, even if they are capable and live near the port of entry. Therefore, they have to hire a customs broker to clear the item. For an inexpensive item, a complex clearance could cost as much as the item. Moreover, can a buyer really shop for and hire a customs broker? Unlikely. More likely, a buyer will use the first customs broker that comes to their attention, one way or another, to do the clearance. This is not a good way to get the lowest cost and the most reliable service. A bad situation!

If this turns out to be the situation, what happens to your feedback? Unhappy buyers do not generate positive feedback.

# The Documents

The commercial invoice is the primary document for customs clearance in the US and Canada. Get it right, and you've done your job as an exporter. For some items, however, other documents may be necessary. For other countries, other documents may be necessary too.

## Commercial Invoice

For a customs invoice you can use either a generic form, a form designed for a more specialized use, or your own invoice. Whatever form you use, it must contain the information outlined below.

Keep in mind that US Customs does not necessarily read the customs invoice for exports. The customs official in the destination country reads it. Consequently, you must comply with that country's regulations. All goods entering the US or Canada must have a commercial invoice that complies with customs regulations.

### Customs Invoices

Note that technically a customs invoice may be required by individual countries. Commercial invoices that satisfy the requirements of customs invoices are accepted as customs invoices.

## Description

The description must describe the item in terms that customs officers can be expected to understand. Avoid industry jargon. Use plain English. But include enough information to adequately identify the item. For instance, include brand names and model numbers, but don't include terms that normal people cannot be expected to understand. *And don't use abbreviations.*

The description is used for classification. The classification determines the duty, if any.

The number of items in the shipment must be stated, too, and all the items must be identical. Any item not identical requires its own description, value, and country of origin.

## Value

Put the value of the item. The value is assumed to be the sales price (transaction price) actually paid. Customs doesn't have to accept your valuation if it seems too low. Customs can make its own valuation regardless of the stated sales price. However, if you can prove your valuation, customs will have to accept it.

## Country of Origin

The country where the item was manufactured must be stated. Are you exporting an item made in India from the US to Canada? Based on the North American Free Trade Agreement (NAFTA), will Canada exclude it from the normal levy of a duty? No. Even though you are exporting it from the US, it was made in India and is subject to any duties Canada levies on goods from India.

### Rules of Origin

Actually, if a product states that it is made in Canada, it may not qualify as a duty-free import into the US (under NAFTA) if it includes parts made in the Philippines (or any other country abroad except Mexico). The rules of origin dictate the origin of the product. If a substantial manufacturing process turns the parts into a finished product, it may qualify as being made in Canada. If a trivial assembling and packaging of the parts constitutes the end product, it may not qualify as being made in Canada.

If you sell goods within the NAFTA countries, the goods may qualify under NAFTA and enter each country duty free. You would need to confer with the NAFTA Rules of Origin to determine if the goods qualify.

## Seller

The seller and the seller's address must be stated. The seller may also be called the *shipper*.

## Buyer

The buyer and the buyer's complete delivery address must be stated. The buyer may also be called the *consignee*.

## NAFTA Statement

If you export from the US to Canada or Mexico, the item will pass through customs duty-free under NAFTA. But you must include a NAFTA statement.

### NAFTA Statement

I certify that the goods described on this invoice originate under the Rules of Origin specified for these goods in the North American Free Trade Agreement and that further production or any operation outside the territories of the Parties has not occurred subsequent to production in the territories.

Name:

Title:

Company:

Status (exporter or producer):

Telephone number:

Fax number:

Country of origin of goods:

Signature:

Date:

For imports over $1,500 CA in Canada and for imports over $2,500 US in the US, a full NAFTA Certificate of Origin including the six-digit Harmonized Tariff number (see Chapter 11) is required, not just a NAFTA statement.

# Certificate of Origin

This is simply a certificate indicating the country where an item was manufactured. It is not an export requirement. It's an import requirement in most countries abroad. It's a standard document which is accepted by most countries.

You don't need this to export from the US to Canada, or vice versa, so long as the NAFTA statement is on the commercial invoice.

## Just Two

For most shipments by eBay businesses to consumers abroad, you need

- A commercial invoice

- A certificate of origin

for all countries except Mexico and Canada where the commercial invoice with a NAFTA statement is sufficient.

## Shipper's Export Declaration

A Shipper's Export Declaration (SED) is a document required by US Customs for exports over $2,500 in value. Many eBay businesses will not have to worry about this. It's strictly a document for a big-ticket item. However, for exports under license, you will have to file a SED regardless of the value.

## Other Documents

Customs can require further documentation according to the laws of the destination country. For instance, US Customs cooperates with other governmental agencies that restrict certain goods (see Chapter 9). Some goods and commodities are regulated and restricted for agricultural protection, safety, or public health and welfare purposes. You may need to supply further documentation to comply with such restrictions. Some goods have import restrictions and quotas designed to protect certain industries. They may require additional documentation too.

## Export Assistance

The Export Assistance Centers around the US will help you with your exporting activities. Keep in mind that the US government wants you to export goods and services. It's good for the national economy. Thus, these offices have been set up with the primary purpose of helping businesses sell abroad. Take advantage of these centers, which the taxpayers have generously dedicated to your benefit.

Associated with the Export Assistance Centers is the monthly publication *Export America* available at the US Government Printing Office (*http://bookstore.gpo.gov*) for $58 annually. Fortunately, you can also find it online at the Export.Gov website (*http://www.export.gov/exportamerica*) and read it each month at no cost.

Assistance with documentation is always a primary concern, and these offices will assist you with any export needs that you have.

### In the US

The government maintains a list of offices to assist you in the US. This list is available at Export.Gov (*http://www.export.gov*) where you can get detailed information on each office including the telephone numbers of staff personnel.

### Abroad

There is a list of offices to assist you abroad with specific countries. Note that many of these international offices cover several countries. This list is available at the BuyUSA.Gov website (*http://www.buyusa.gov/home/worldwide_us.html*) where you can get detailed information on each office.

## Foreign Consular Offices

The US Department of State maintains a list of foreign consulates in the US. For instance, a foreign country may have a number of consulates in cities around the US. You can see the list at *http://*

*www.state.gov/s/cpr/rls/fco*. These offices are a place to get information on the documents required at customs in a particular country.

## Forms and Samples

Forms and samples for customs documents are readily available many places on the Web. The couriers offer forms and samples on their websites together with explanations making it easy for you to draft the documents. Ron's customs brokerage firm has forms on its website at *http://www.aacb.com*. And the customs websites have forms too. As you have read in this chapter, however, you don't necessarily need to use a form for every document so long as your own versions of the documents contain all the necessary information.

## Placement

The customs invoice goes in an envelope marked *customs documents* attached to the outside of the package. Remember, the letter will be opened by customs. Consequently, you also need to put a shipping label elsewhere on the package.

The couriers will supply a pouch on the package for the customs documents. In a bulk shipment, the customs documents are normally attached to the waybill.

# Your Role

Your obligation as the seller is not to clear an item through customs. Rather, it's to provide complete documentation acceptable to customs.

## Buyer's Obligation

It's the buyer's obligation to clear an item through customs. But the buyer is stuck with whatever paperwork comes with the item being imported. If your paperwork is proper and complete, the buyer's import will presumably be trouble free. If not, you may have a dissatisfied customer on your hands.

Good documentation makes for clear sailing. Poor documentation, if the item gets as far as customs, is likely to cause delays, require professional assistance, and cost the buyer more.

### Auction Ad

You might want to put a URL in your auction ads to help potential buyers abroad prepare for clearing items through customs in their own countries. A good one would be the World Customs Organization (*http://www.wcoomd.org/ie/index.html*) where buyers abroad can go to get customs information on their own countries.

## Change in Obligations

The buyer and seller can agree on a change in the obligations. For instance, the seller can agree to clear the goods through customs in the country where the buyer resides at the seller's cost.

Indeed, buyers may not be familiar with import-export procedures. It's really in the best interest of the seller to instruct the buyer what the procedures are and who is obligated to do what. Otherwise, a buyer who doesn't understand may file negative feedback, particularly when his or her lack of action (out of ignorance) has an adverse affect on the shipment. Or, for premium customer service, the seller can do the clearance. Usually, that means hiring a customs broker at seller's expense to work under the seller's management.

### Best Way

The best way to handle clearing customs is to provide door-to-door fret-free delivery service or cross-border warehousing as mentioned in Chapters 8 and 27. This takes the burden off buyers and puts it on sellers. Great customer service!

Sellers should state in their eBay auction ads who needs to do what, when, where, and an estimate of what it will cost.

# Physical Inspection

US Customs officials do physical inspections of goods and containers too, although as mentioned at the beginning of the chapter, they can't inspect everything.. We're not concerned about physical inspections because we have nothing to hide. However, if you think you can put something illegal past an inspector, you may be unpleasantly surprised. Then too, consider that inspections are tightening up in the age of terrorism.

# Summary

For most eBay consumer exports, a complete commercial invoice and a certificate of origin are what you need to make sure that the item can be imported by the buyer easily and at the lowest cost. Get set up to produce customs invoices automatically (digitally) that are complete and effective, and you will become a competent exporter.

For great customer service, sellers should consider taking on the buyer's clearance tasks to provide fret-free door-to-door delivery.

# 7

# *Import and Export Licenses*

Do you need a license to be in the import-export business in the US? Absolutely not, with certain exceptions. And those exceptions are reasonably narrow. Generally, goods requiring an export license are arms, some high-tech products that could be used against the US, and certain strategic goods temporarily restricted. Generally, goods requiring an import license are drugs, arms, and alcoholic beverages, the same goods for which you need a license to sell in the US. The vast majority of US eBay retailers will not have to worry about import-export licensing in the US. Consequently we can keep this chapter short.

# Exporting

For explicit information on export licensing, check the Export Administration Regulations published by the Bureau of Industry and Security, formerly the Bureau of Export Administration (BXA) under the Department of Commerce. You can find it the Bureau's website at *http://www.bxa.doc.gov.* You can also get information on exports at Export.Gov (*http://export.gov/exportcontrols.html*).

The first step in determining whether you need a license to export certain goods is to classify the goods with an Export Control Classification Number (ECCN). If indeed there is a classification that matches a description of your goods, the goods may come under the export licensing regulations. If not, you don't need a license.

The categories of goods and materials requiring a license include:

- Nuclear materials
- Certain chemicals, microorganisms, and toxins
- Electronic equipment
- Computers
- Telecommunications
- Information security
- Sensors and lasers
- Navigation and avionics devices
- Marine systems
- Propulsion systems and space vehicles

Again, the above categories include primarily goods that are weapons or technology that can be used against the US. Few consumer items fall under the above categories. To learn more go to the regulations database at *http://w3.access.gpo.gov/bis/ear/ear_data.html*.

Note that certain licenses are country-specific. In other words, you may need a license to export to one country but not another. Indeed, countries on unfriendly terms with the US may require import-export licensing for anything. They include: Cambodia, Cuba, Iran, Libya, and North Korea. Note also you will need to file a Shipper's Export Declaration (SED) for exports under license regardless of value. See Chapter 6.

Our experience indicates that the only category that eBay retailers should worry about is perhaps computers. You may be selling a digital product that requires a license. For instance, encryption software is one thing you will want to thoroughly check before you sell it outside the US.

For information on exporting from Canada, check International Trade Canada at *http://www.dfait-maeci.gc.ca/trade/menu-en.asp*, and Strategis (*http://strategis.ic.gc.ca*).

# Importing

For importing, you will need licenses similar to licenses you need to sell the goods in the US. Such goods include drugs, weapons, and alcohol for consumption. So, yes, for such goods you need an import license, and yes, you need another license in the US to sell such goods.

# Quotas

Certain goods are restricted for import by quotas. In order to import such goods, you must have a license for each specific shipment. The license is not issued in the US but rather in the country of origin on a first-come-first-served basis. If the quota for that country has been filled, you're out of luck. In other words, if you want to import 1,000 Madras shirts from India, which will come into the US under a textile quota, you will have to get a license from India to import the shirts into the US.

Note that textile quotas are common and perhaps the most likely quotas that eBay businesses will have to worry about. The best way to avoid serious problems with your clothing (or other goods under quota) is to discuss your anticipated clothing import activities with a customs broker before you attempt to import anything. (Note, also, in 2005 the textile quotas will lifted under a new WTO agreement.)

# Restricted Goods

Do not mistake the fact that you don't need a license to import something to mean that such goods have no restrictions. There are a wide range of goods subject to import restrictions and quotas. See more in Chapter 9.

# Licenses Abroad

Unfortunately, we can't say much about licenses abroad except to note that there are as many different licensing requirements as there are countries. Most countries won't require individuals to get a license to import one consumer item or even a small number of consumer items. For items in bulk, however, which you will store in a warehouse and distribute, a country may require a license. As part of your investigation on a country regarding sales tax, value added tax (VAT), and duties, you need to obtain information on licensing too.

# Summary

US licensing isn't a big issue in consumer import-export and in most eBay import-export. Nonetheless, understand that the notion of national security is behind most US export licensing and the notion of normal controls is behind most US import licensing.

Licensing by countries abroad in conjunction with US trade quotas is a requirement that some eBay businesses will face.

# 8

## *Customs Brokers and Freight Forwarders*

Most eBay businesses will need assistance, not just expertise, when they import and export. That is, few eBay businesses will develop the staff in-house to clear items through customs. More likely they will turn to a customs broker or a freight forwarder (shipping agent) to do the clearance on their behalf. This is a cost-effective means to complete a complex task necessary in the import-export business.

The key to cost-effectiveness is to anticipate when and where you will need a customs broker or freight forwarder and to line one up ahead of time. This not only gives you time to discuss fees and service requirements but, more importantly, to discuss your business plans and objectives and to understand the problems you may face in moving your goods across borders. A customs broker or freight forwarder can be a useful resource and assist you in gaining a competitive advantage in the marketplace.

# Definitions

To start the chapter, it is useful to provide simple definitions of customs brokers and freight forwarders.

## Customs Broker

A customs broker is a firm that provides trained personnel to take your item and clear it through customs. Customs brokers are familiar with the customs laws of the country in which they operate. However, beyond that they are familiar with all laws that affect importing such as import quotas and restrictions, laws that promote health, welfare, safety, and national defense and how such laws relate to the clearance process. Naturally, they know all the forms and how to find and fill in the requisite information for customs and the various agencies. Indeed, their primary job is to process the paperwork on behalf of the importer (usually a buyer) in conjunction with customs officials. Customs brokers are normally licensed by the country in which they work.

Legally, a customs broker acts as an agent on behalf of the importer of record by representing the importer with customs in the country into which the goods are imported. Hiring a customs broker can be an important component of your importing strategy.

## *Freight Forwarder*

It's usually not enough to put a shipment on a ship or an airplane. Few factories are at the airport or at the dock. A freight forwarder is a firm that specializes in handling the shipping from a factory in one country to a warehouse in another country or even to a consumer (buyer). That shipping may start out by truck, go on a train, be loaded on a ship, and then go on a truck. In other words, the shipment is handled by several shippers on the way to its destination. The freight forwarder usually manages the process on behalf of the importer in the destination country or on behalf of the exporter in the country of origin. (See Incoterms in Chapter 21 regarding the responsibilities of buyers and sellers.) Part of that process is obtaining insurance for the shipment.

Freight forwarders are particularly important for less-than-container-load shipments. They assemble, collect, consolidate, and ship goods from multiple sources. Consequently, an importer gets a less expensive shipping rate than otherwise using an entire container.

Freight forwarders are familiar with the import and export rules and regulations of both the country of origin and the destination country. The can also advise on the best method of shipping and cost-saving and are familiar with the import-export documentation. Thus, using a freight forwarder can be very cost-effective.

Freight forwarders have also been known as shipping agents and freight consolidators.

# Realities

Firms representing the traditional definitions of customs brokers and freight forwarders can still be found today, but the greater reality is that many such firms have evolved into offering a wide range of services. Consequently, it's often difficult to tell the difference between the leading customs brokers and freight forwarders.

In choosing a customs broker or freight forwarder, you will want to find one that offers appropriate services to the type of importing or exporting you are doing. For instance, some specialize in North America, some in other areas, and some in special types of goods.

# Services

The modern customs brokers and freight forwarders offer a variety of services. By managing the shipping process from beginning to end, they can create efficiencies and save time making their services well worth the cost.

## Customs Brokers Evolve

You can see from the definitions above that a customs broker can probably do its job more efficiently if it has control over the entire process of shipping and customs clearance. In fact, the customs broker can anticipate the necessary documents that must accompany a shipment and make sure its customer, the importer, generates all the proper paperwork even before shipment.

Specialties develop within the customs broker's firm between customs brokerage and freight forwarding. The customs broker can then offer a full range of services. The buyer, the importer, then gets one-stop service. The importer need only deal with one firm, a modern customs broker.

## Freight Forwarders Evolve

You can also see from the definitions above that the freight forwarder has a serious potential bottleneck in the shipping process. That is, the customs clearance. A freight forwarder can do its job for an importer more efficiently if it does the customs clearance as well as manages the shipping process.

Specialties develop within the freight forwarding firm between freight forwarding and customs brokerage, and the freight forwarder can then offer a full range of services. The buyer, the importer, then gets one-stop service. The importer need only deal with one firm, a modern freight forwarder.

### In Other Words

In other words, there is little difference between the leading customs brokers and the leading freight forwarders today. But before you hire a firm, make sure you know what services they provide that you need and what services they don't provide that you may need.

## Consulting

Once you have hired a firm to handle the process of shipping and clearing customs for you, the firm can take control and streamline the entire process. This makes a lot of sense. In cases where the importing is an ongoing activity, a modern customs broker or freight forwarder can offer you advice on and develop strategies for reducing costs, increasing security, and expediting the movement of goods. This makes a lot of sense compared to having several different firms provide services and solutions to problems piecemeal.

## Payment

Naturally, when clearing customs, you often have to pay duties. If your customs broker or freight forwarder pays for you, that removes one of the bureaucratic steps that potentially might cause a delay. To get such financial service, however, you must have good credit, and you usually get billed immediately.

## Warehousing

Another service that may be provided by customs brokers and freight forwarders is warehousing. First, your shipment may need bonded warehousing. That is, it needs to go somewhere immediately until customs clearance is complete. The warehouse bonds (segregates) goods for which duty is not yet paid. As the goods are sold, the duties are paid, and the goods are released from the warehouse.

Another type of storage is cross-border warehousing. This is a great technique for eBay importers and exporters and is a little different than a bonded warehouse. Read more about import warehousing in Chapter 27.

## *For Example*

What can customs brokers and freight forwarders do for you? Here are some examples:

- Ship Chinese imports through Canada, where taxes and duties are paid, to the US where the taxes and duties must be paid again. Then get a refund from Canada.

- Ship Chinese imports into Canada leaving part of the shipment in bond (duty-free), which is then shipped on to the US.

- Arrange for Pre-Arrival Release System (PARS) truck shipments from the US into Canada. The trucks clear customs easily with no delay.

- Arrange for US exporters to be Non-Resident Importers (NRI) in Canada through a special process. This works well for eBay businesses. See Chapter 27.

- Provide door-to-door transport service that is great for sellers as well as great customer service for buyers abroad.

- Completely relieve you of doing the research and paperwork necessary to effectively, efficiently, and cost-effectively import and export in regard to your eBay business.

There are many more examples of effort-saving and cost-saving processes that a customs broker or freight forwarder can provide for you.

### Substitute?

Can you substitute your own effort for that of a customs broker or freight forwarder? If you live near the port of entry and are willing to develop the expertise and put forth the effort, the answer is, yes. Few of us are in that position, however, and it's more cost-effective to hire a customs broker or a freight forwarder.

Keep in mind, too, that the post office in the US and Canada will clear an item under a threshold amount for a small fee.

# Directories

The following are directories where you can find customs brokers and freight forwarders to assist you in your eBay business. Remember, if you make arrangements in advance, you will have time to investigate the scope of services available and to negotiate fees.

- Canadian International Freight Forwarders Association (CIFFA), *http://www.ciffa.com/regmem.asp?usedb=REGURegularMembers&mt=1*, gives a list of freight forwarders in Canada.

- Canadian Society of Customs Brokers, *http://www.cscb.ca/directory/direct.htm*, provides a list of Canadian customs brokers.

- Freightgate, *http://www.freightgate.com/directories/directories.tet*, provides a directory for customs brokers, freight forwarders, and other import-export service companies worldwide.

- International Federation of Customs Brokers Associations (IFCBA), *http://www.ifcba.org/members.htm*, publishes a list of nation members worldwide. Web links to national members will eventually get you to online national membership directories.

- National Customs Brokers & Forwarders Association of America (NCBFAA), *http://www.ncbfaa.org/scripts/search.asp*, gives you a searchable membership directory.

Don't overlook A&A Contract Customs Brokers, Ltd. (*http://www.aacb.com*), a Canadian customs broker for which Ron works and which has been a participant at the first three eBay annual conferences in Anaheim, Orlando, and New Orleans. A&A has an office in the US which extends its services to a second country.

# Couriers

What we know as FedEx and UPS in the US are known as *couriers* internationally. They are limited in the size of freight they can carry due to operational requirements. But they typically act like freight forwarders, in effect.

The couriers pick up packages in a truck;

Put the packages on an airplane;

Fly them to a central hub where the packages are sorted;

Put them on another airplane;

Fly them to the destination country;

Take them off the airline at the destination;

And put them on a truck for delivery.

But they have to clear packages through customs too. They have their own set of US Customs officials at their central hub where all packages enter the US. And they work with the customs officials at airports abroad. They clear items through customs for buyers (consignees) for a fee.

### Ground Service

The couriers also offer ground transportation across the US-Canadian border, an inexpensive means of shipping.

# Post Offices

The post offices, of course, occupy a unique place in each country as they are governmental institutions. Therefore, they have a special relationship with customs. Like the couriers, they act like freight forwarders, in effect. Post offices pick up packages and fly them to a destination abroad. Thereafter, they have no control. However, with postal treaties they have relationships and agreements with the post offices in countries abroad. The post office in the destination country completes the shipping process by clearing the goods through customs and by providing shipment to the final destination. In many cases, this is the most cost-effective means of shipping inexpensive consumer items globally. However, don't expect the quality of service to be on a par with the couriers. Postal shipments tend to take longer than courier shipments, often significantly longer.

For instance, for a $5 CA fee, the Canada Post will have customs clear a package so long as the value is less than $1,600 CA. In the US for shipments under $2,000 US in value, the Postal Service will have customs clear a package for a $5 US fee. Most countries will clear a package shipped via the post office for an administrative fee.

# Customer Service

Let's not forget customer service. If you sell an item to a person abroad, wouldn't it be great customer service to have the package arrive at their doorstep without any effort or additional payment on their part? A customs broker, freight forwarder, courier, or post office can make that happen for you as the seller for the benefit of your customer, the buyer. Great customer service!

This type of service is becoming the norm rather than the exception. As the import-export industry services consolidate to offer one-stop service, eBay sellers can offer customers abroad a fret-free door-to-door service, albeit at a higher purchase price. The purchase price has to cover the door-to-door service.

## Summary

Although the most cost-effective way to ship most individual items to another country is via the post office, you need to familiarize yourself with the various services available from the US Postal Service or Canada Post in regard to shipping to make sure you get the service you need. For high-value items, multiple items, safer service, or faster service, you may find a courier, freight forwarder, or customs broker more cost-effective.

# *9*

# *Restricted Imports and Exports*

As reviewed in Chapter 7, certain narrow categories of goods require that you have an import or export license. But, although licensing is generally irrelevant to eBay retailing, restrictions are not. Many goods are restricted based on a whole range of health, welfare, safety, taxation, and political issues. In order to deal in restricted goods, you must comply with the requisite regulations.

The restrictions on goods being imported into the US are not necessarily customs restrictions. They can be any restrictions imposed by such federal agencies as the Department of Agriculture, Food and

Drug Administration, and the Department of Energy, to mention a few. Note, too, that some goods are restricted by an import quota or a restraint in a trade agreement.

The laws and regulations regarding restricted goods are usually enforced by US Customs in conjunction with the governmental agencies that administer such laws and regulations.

# Restricted for Import

The following is a list of goods restricted by various government agencies upon import. The US Customs on behalf of the agencies requires that you comply with the restrictions of the various agencies in the import process. This usually requires extra paperwork.

List of restricted goods and materials:

- Dairy products
- Fruit, vegetables, and nuts
- Plants
- Seeds
- Poultry
- Livestock and animals
- Meat
- Food
- Alcohol
- Arms and explosives
- Radioactive materials
- Radiation products
- Radio frequency products

- Machine tools

- Household appliances

- Flammable fabrics

- Motor vehicles

- Boats

- Money

- Gold and silver

- Postage stamps

- Biological materials and drugs

- Narcotics

- Cosmetics

- Textiles

- Wool or fur

- Petroleum products

- Pesticides

- Toxic or hazardous substances

- Trademarked and copyrighted materials

- Pornography

- Counterfeit items

- Products manufactured in certain countries

- Products made with forced labor

List of goods with quotas:

- Milk and cream

- Anchovies

- Olives

- Tuna fish

- Whiskbrooms

- Textiles (to be eliminated in 2005)

- Alcohol

- Animal feed

- Butter

- Peanuts

- Cotton

- Sugar blends

- Watch movements

This is not a complete list nor a current list, but it gives you an idea of the types of goods that are restricted. Perhaps the easiest-to-use general guide to restricted imports is one for travelers at US Customs & Border Protection (*http://www.customs.gov/xp/cgov/travel/leavingarrivinginUS/vacation/know_brochure/prohibited_restricted.xml*). Use this for a general overview but note that the exemptions for travelers don't apply to importers.

You can find out more about importing restricted goods at the International Trade Data System website (*http://www.itds.treas.gov/specimpreq.html*).

For Canada, you can get a list of OGDs at *http://www.cbsa-asfc.gc.ca/import/otherdepartments-e.html*. OGD stands for Other Goverment Department referring to Canadian goverment departments that have import restrictions.

### Prohibitions

Note that some items are prohibited completely from being imported. That's the ultimate restriction.

Clearance is given by US Customs only if the requirements by other governmental agencies are met. Keep in mind, too, that these restrictions have nothing to do with the mode of transportation. They apply to all goods, including ones shipped via the post office.

### Good News or Bad News?

The good news for US citizens is that the government is protecting you against terrorism by restricting food imports. The bad news is that this restriction makes importing food into the US an extra burden now. The restriction applies to all food, even a birthday cake from your aunt in Canada.

# Restricted for Export

The goods restricted for export from the US are covered in Chapter 7. Check International Trade Canada (*http://www.dfait-maeci.gc.ca/ trade/menu-en.asp*) and Strategis (*http://strategis.ic.gc.ca*) for Canadian export information.

# Rules and Regulations

If you have a need to reference the US Customs rules and regulations, go to US Customs & Border Protection, *http://www.customs.treas.gov*, an agency of the Department of Homeland Security.

For Canada go to Canada Border Services Agency (CBSA), *http:// www.cbsa-asfc.gc.ca/menu.html*.

For other countries go to the World Customs Organization (WCO) at *http://www.wcoomd.org/ie/index.html*.

# Plan Ahead

If you deal in restricted goods, you have a lot of planning to do. You need to develop a strategy to meet all the regulations of every governmental agency necessary to get your goods cleared. You must get this done systematically so that your goods don't get bogged down in the customs bureaucracy. For instance, hiring a customs broker can be of invaluable assistance in getting the job done.

A good example is textiles, which is on both the restricted list and the quotas list. That means if you import clothes, you may have a problem getting your clothes cleared, unless you take the necessary steps to make sure you can satisfy all the requirements for clearance.

In the case of clothing, you don't want to be surprised. The restrictions apply to clothing packages shipped via the post office or any other way. You need to work with a customs broker to anticipate what requirements you will have to meet, how you will meet them, and how to keep up with current developments (e.g., textiles will be not be on quotas in 2005 under a new WTO agreement).

# Summary

Unfortunately, the laws and regulations pertaining to restricted goods are often complex and possibly administered by several different govermental agencies. If you want to import such goods you have to make sure you can meet all the requirements for import. Customs will not allow your restricted goods to clear otherwise.

Nonetheless, these restrictions present an opportunity too. Only those with the fortitude to move such goods through customs will be able to import and sell such goods in the US. Such restrictions will have the effect of thinning out the competition and possibly giving you a competitive edge.

# III

## *Finance*

# *10*

## *Taxes on Sales*

In the US, we understand sales tax. A sales tax is collected by a state on all products sold within the state. There are only about five states that don't have a sales tax. If you sell something on eBay to a resident in your own state (where your business is located), you have to collect sales tax on the item from the buyer (e.g., about 8 percent in California). If you sell something to a customer residing outside your own state, you don't have to collect sales tax on it.

In the US we don't have a value-added tax (VAT). This is a common tax, however, in other countries. Sometimes it is a substitute for an income tax. Sometimes it is in addition to an income tax. It is similar to a sales tax except that it is usually collected by the national government. It is another tax paid when something is purchased. In Canada, for instance, it's known as the Goods and Services Tax (GST).

# Sales Tax

Sales tax is collected by many countries but not by the US.

## *In the US*

In the US, the federal government never gets involved in the collection of sales tax. It is a tax charged by a state, and it is up to the state to collect it. Let's say you are an eBay business in Mississippi, and you sell something to a Mississippi resident. Mississippi expects you to collect sales tax from the buyer and pay it to the state. If you don't, you are subject to both civil and criminal penalties. That means Mississippi potentially can collect the money (the tax amount) from you and perhaps send you to prison too.

Let's say you sell something to a buyer in the state of Arizona. Mississippi can't collect Arizona sales tax. The purchase is deemed to be made in Arizona where the buyer resides. Mississippi has no interest in collecting Arizona's sales tax. Thus, when you sell something to a buyer residing in Arizona, it is essentially sales-tax-free. Theoretically, the buyer should pay sales tax to Arizona, but who does that? How can that be enforced?

The item purchased never passes through a state border customs station. There are no customs between states in the US. The state of Arizona never knows about the purchase of the item.

### Large Catalog Sellers

Certain large catalog sellers have facilities in many states and therefore cannot get out of collecting sales tax on their sales in those states. Some even have facilities in every state.

## *In Other Countries*

Don't expect things to be the same in other countries. For instance in Canada, the Canadian federal government collects not only the GST federal tax but also provincial sales tax (PST) on products coming into the country. That's a good deal for the provinces. Were it not for Canadian Customs, a province would not know about the purchase and would be unable to collect the sales tax. This is a simple concept, right? Not exactly.

If an item comes into a Canadian port of entry in the province of British Columbia on its way to a buyer in the province of Ontario, the federal government doesn't collect the sales tax for Ontario. The federal customs station is in British Columbia and collects only British Columbia sales tax. There are other complexities in the Canadian sales tax system too.

As a Mississippi eBay business, can you plan on selling something to a Canadian buyer with the certainty that the buyer will not have to pay sales tax? Unlikely. You would have to control the shipment completely and make sure it goes through the proper port of entry to avoid the sales tax.

### *Taxes*

The GST and PST are not import taxes and are not necessarily an impediment to importing goods. They are collected on domestic goods as well.

## *So What?*

So, what difference does it make to you as a Mississippi eBay business if a foreign country collects sales tax? Perhaps none. But let's look at that a little closer.

A strong advantage the catalog industry in the US has had for many decades is that buyers generally don't pay sales tax on the items they buy in catalogs. They do pay shipping. This is often a wash in buyers' minds. "I don't have to pay sales tax, but I do have to pay shipping. And I come out about the same as buying in a local store." This advantage has been continued on the Web. Web sales, whether on eBay or in another Web marketplace, are like catalog sales.

If that advantage is not available to your sales efforts in another country (i.e., if the buyer has to pay sales tax), it may have an effect on your sales to buyers in that country. How detrimental that effect will be to your sales effort, if at all, is difficult to judge, but it's something you will want to consider.

In a place like Canada where everyone expects to pay GST and PST all the time, it may not make any difference. But at the same time, the cost of shipping from the US and the customs duties, if any, may become the difference that dampens sales. Since such costs are not offset by the non-payment of taxes in Canada, as they are in the US, the shipping expense and duties may discourage sales.

# Value-Added Tax

The way a VAT works in theory is that in each transfer of the product where value is added—from the raw materials to the final product—the added value is taxed. The last transfer is to the consumer. It is the retailer that adds the last value by the process of marketing and selling the product. Suppose the retailer's cost of a product is $50. The retailer sells it to a consumer for $90. The VAT is paid on the difference of $40 ($90 − $50 = $40), the amount of value the retailer added.

For that product, the making of the raw materials was subject to VAT. The manufacturing of the product was subject to VAT. The warehousing and distribution (wholesaling) was subject to VAT. And finally the retailing was subject to VAT and paid by the consumer.

## US VAT

In the US you don't have to worry about VAT. There is no VAT, although certain politicians have proposed a VAT to replace the income tax.

## VAT Countries

In countries that have VAT, guess what's likely to happen to products that you sell to consumers in those countries? The products get taxed by the VAT. It's likely to be for the entire value of the product, the sales price.

For instance, as a Mississippi eBay business, if you sell an item to a consumer in Canada, the item will be taxed 7 percent GST (a VAT) on the sales price of the item by the Canadian federal government as it enters the country.

VATs are a popular taxing method, and many countries use them. Canada has an income tax, so the Canadian VAT is a supplementary tax to the income tax. In countries without income tax, the VAT percentage is likely to be higher than 7 percent. For the European Common Market, the minimum VAT is 15 percent, although countries can charge more if they choose. Indeed, the European VATs range from 15 to 25 percent.

## So What? Again

So, what difference does it make to you as a Mississippi eBay business if a foreign country collects VAT? Perhaps none. But again let's look at that a little closer.

In Canada, a buyer has to pay a 7 percent VAT as well as a provincial sales tax, another 7 or 8 percent (except in Alberta). That's a total of 15 percent tax on the sale that the buyer must pay, and we haven't even talked about duties that may have to be paid too. (See Chapter 11 for a discussion of import duties.) This 15 percent taxation could be a disincentive to purchase. It's difficult to tell.

An item that might look good to someone in Arizona who pays no sales tax buying from an eBay business in Mississippi might not look as good to a Canadian who must pay 15 percent tax buying from the Mississippi eBay business. That will depend on the item and the price. Again, the disincentive becomes the shipping cost and the duties, if any; and the shipping cost and duties are not balanced by the non-payment of taxes as in the US.

The one thing that the Mississippi eBay seller has going for it in this scenario is that consumers in other countries expect to pay the VAT and the sales tax on anything they buy. It's built into their expectations just like state sales tax in the US is built into the purchasing expectations of consumers at the local mall. So, you can make the claim that VAT should not have an effect on marketing, and there's a lot to that.

Nonetheless, it's hard to believe an extra 15 or 25 percent to pay for an item will have absolutely no effect on marketing.

The worst case for the Mississippi eBay business is not to know about VAT and other consumer taxes in a country where it expects to get a lot of business. Just knowing about the tax situation in a country can make the difference between a good marketing plan and one that fails.

## VAT Refunds

When you purchase goods abroad and are required to pay VAT, you may be eligible for a refund. If you are not a resident of the country and if you do not have a place of business in the country, you usually do not have to pay VAT. Consequently, if you are required to pay it when making a purchase, you can later apply for a refund.

There are firms that actually manage your VAT refund applications for you. The VAT laws can be complex, and such firms are experts in value-added taxation. Unless you are a huge company, it's probably more cost-effective for you to have one of these firms make your refund applications than do it yourself. For small eBay businesses, using one of these firms just may be too expensive, although some of the firms advertise that they will even help tourists recover VAT on their tourist purchases.

Global Refund (*http://www.globalrefund.com*)

International Sales Tax Refund Corporation (*http://www.insatax.com*)

Numerica (*http://www.numerica.biz/servicesvatservices.asp*)

Vatcollect (*http://www.vatcollect.com*)

Let's say you buy a closeout in France on 2,000 sets of kitchen storage containers for $15,000 and pay the VAT. Is it worth it to apply for a refund? Yes. France has a VAT of about 20 percent. Your refund would be $3,000.

# Excise Tax

This is a tax levied on the sale of a specific product designated to receive special tax treatment by a country. For instance, luxuries often have excise taxes (e.g., wine and liquor, jewelry, ). The excise taxes and the products they cover will vary from country to country. Again we have exactly the same problem as with the other taxes. The person in the country with the excise tax will pay more for the item. How does this affect your marketing effort? Is it important to know?

Canada has excise taxes on a number of products. When you add VAT, sales tax, and excise tax together, the sales taxation starts to look rather high. Of course, there are excise taxes in the US too.

Because excise taxes by definition are levied only on certain goods, not all goods, the complexities generated by 200 different countries are staggering. This is information you use by reference only. That's why a trade reference system for your office is important (see Chapter 4).

# Complexity

Thus far we have discussed buyers in Canada. We have used an example of a US seller in Mississippi selling to consumers abroad. The complexities of these taxes in Canada are more extensive than we're revealing—after all this isn't a taxation book. And there are about 200 other countries, each with their own tax complexities. It's a daunting task to keep track of it all.

You shouldn't have to keep track of it all. That's what a trade reference system is for. What you do need to do is use your reference information when you plan a marketing campaign in a particular country. It's crucial to know how much consumers in that country will actually have to pay (after tax) for your products.

For a list of VAT, sales tax, and duties in each country, see:

United States Council for International Business (*http://www.uscib.org/index.asp?documentID=1676*)

# Summary

It's easy to stick your head in the sand when you're a seller and ignore taxes. After all, it's the buyer who pays taxes in her own country on her purchases. That's a short-sighted way to do business, however, and you need to be conscious of what buyers in different countries face. It affects your marketing and sales strategies.

When you are a buyer in another country and pay taxes, you may be able to get refunds on the VAT paid. The VAT can be a substantial percentage, leading to a substantial refund.

# *11*

# *Import Duties*

All countries tax imports. The import tax or duty is not uniform, however, and you have to determine what the duty is. Countries don't necessarily tax imports to raise money, although that is certainly a desirable objective. Rather, they tax imports to protect local manufacturers from foreign competition. Because the duty is not uniform, you need to research the duty for each item you import. There are four questions to ask:

1. Is there a minimum value exemption?

2. Is there an exemption due to a trade treaty?

3. Is there an exemption for the type of goods?

4. If there is no exemption, what is the duty?

If you are the importer, the determination of the duty is something you have to know. After all, the duty can be a major expense. This is particularly important when you import in bulk. The duty, if too high, can break the success of an import plan.

Keep in mind, however, that the determination of the duty is important when you export too, for the reasons stated in Chapter 10. You need to know what duty your eBay customer has to pay on an item in order to develop an effective marketing plan.

# Minimum Exemption

Many countries have a minimum threshold of value before the payment of duty is required. For instance, in Canada it's $20 CA and in the US it's $200 US. Anything less than $20 in value can be imported into Canada with out paying duty, and anything less than $200 US in value can be imported into the US without paying duty. The minimums around the globe can help to inspire a lot of eBay commerce. But they will be different from country to country.

### Exemptions Don't Apply

Exemptions don't apply to restricted goods. For restricted goods, you may still have to deal with other government departments as discussed in Chapter 9.

# Trade Treaty Exemption

In some cases, trade treaties do away with duties. For example, the North American Free Trade Agreement (NAFTA) is a treaty between the US, Canada, and Mexico that eliminates duties between those countries. The European Union (Common Market) is another example. It has eliminated duties between its member countries. In fact, NAFTA was created as a competitive reaction to the European Union.

NAFTA creates a "common market" between its three member countries just like the European Union creates a common market between certain European countries. Consequently, anything imported into the US from Canada or Mexico is duty-free. If you're an eBay business in Mississippi, you don't have to worry about duties when you sell to buyers in Canada or Mexico.

Under NAFTA, not all goods are duty free. You still have to meet the NAFTA rules of origin, which have to do with where an item is actually manufactured. If it was manufactured in the US, Canada, or Mexico, it's duty-free. If it was manufactured in another country (e.g., Peru), you would not be able to export it from the US to Canada, for example, duty-free.

# Product Exemption

When a country establishes customs duties (a tariff is a list of duties), it does not necessarily do so for all goods. It may levy duties only on the goods of local industries it wants to protect from global competition. For instance, a steel-producing country may levy a duty on imported steel. It might charge a duty that puts imported steel on a price-parity with foreign steel, or it might charge a duty so high that it gives local steel a price advantage. On the other hand, a country may decide not to levy a duty on a foreign product that it wants to be imported and that doesn't compete with any domestic product. This is all politics. Politics is a very complex process, and the tariffs of every country seem to reflect politics. That is, the tariffs are complex.

# Calculating the Duty

Calculating the duty for a product is not a calculating process alone. It's a classification process first. Mathematical calculations are exact, but classifications are open to interpretation. Accordingly, calculated duties are never certain until customs makes its determination.

# Classification

As you can imagine, there are thousands of different types of raw materials and products that are imported. There are correspondingly thousands of classifications.

## Self-Classification

If you want to estimate the duty to be paid when your imported product passes through customs, your first task is to place it in the appropriate classification. How do you do this?

Well, you can gaze through the Harmonized Tariff Schedule of the US (*http://www.usitc.gov/taffairs.htm*). You can purchase a copy from the US Government Printing Office (GPO – *http://www.gpoaccess.gov*) for $65 on CD. It is issued twice a year, and the $65 covers two issues. You can find Canadian tariffs at *http://www.cbsa-asfc.gc.ca/general/publications/tariff2004/tablewithamendments-e.html*.

Once you determine the classification, you can calculate the duty. The US levies different duties on different classifications, as does Canada.

The Harmonized System (HS) also known as the Harmonized Commodity Description and Coding System is an international product-description scheme developed by the World Customs Organization. It is made up of about 5,000 commodity groups, each identified by a six-digit code. The system is used by over 190 countries including the US and Canada. Each country ads two or four digits to the code for their own use. Each country bases their tariff schedules (duties) on the HS. The HS provides duties for virtually every item that exists.

Customs brokers have years of experience in properly classifying goods. Classification can be very specific in detail. A proper and complete classification is required to apply the correct duty to an item.

### Customs Classification

Naturally, customs isn't obligated to accept your classification. It can make its own determination. If your product is placed in a class requiring the payment of higher duties, your imports will cost more than you had estimated. Sometimes the classification is the most crucial step in the process and foments substantial disagreement between an importer and customs. Of course, this is not an dispute an importer is likely to win.

Nonetheless, note that the World Reference mentioned in Chapter 4 provides a searchable database of 86,000 US Customs rulings. If you can consult the rulings, you may find grounds to change minds at US Customs. You can also find Canadian customs rulings online at *http:// www.cbsa-asfc.gc.ca/E/pub/cm/d11-11-2/d11112-e.pdf.*

## Calculate the Duty

The value of the imported products is the sales price. Once you classify the products, you consult the Harmonized Tariff Schedule for the amount of the duty (a percentage) and calculate by multiplying the percentage times the transaction price. Quite simple really! Unfortunately, customs doesn't have to accept your sales price. If the price doesn't look right, customs can appraise the products using one of several appraisal methods.

A new appraisal can compound a misclassification. If customs both classifies your products and appraises them differently, the duties you have to pay may be substantially different than you anticipated.

## Risk

What's the risk of different customs classifications and appraisals ruining your estimates? It depends on how careful you do your research. Most of the time if you classify competently, your classifications will hold up. If the sales prices are reasonable according to market norms, they will undoubtedly stick. So, there are not necessarily any stumbling blocks in the process of determining duties. But sometimes things work out differently than you anticipated.

You can see that your trade reference system (see Chapter 4) can be very helpful here. The more information you have at your fingertips, the more likely you will be able to work efficiently and therefore inexpensively.

## Pay the Duty

US Customs will not accept payment of duties in advance. Once customs makes its determinations, you pay the duties. When the customs determinations are final, they are deemed to be *liquidated*. Upon liquidation, you pay the duties.

What happens if you don't pay the duties? The products are subject to confiscation by US Customs.

## Brokers and Freight Forwarders

Now, it's one thing to make estimates of duties to be paid for the purpose of projecting business costs. It's another to actually take the products through the customs procedures. You need a customs broker or a freight forwarder to do that. See Chapter 8 for more information on these services.

## In Other Countries

In other countries, the classifications and duties are different. As a practical matter, unless you're selling in heavy volume around the globe, you can't take the time and effort to do the research to make accurate estimates of the duties your customers abroad will pay. Nonetheless, if you find that a high percentage of your orders are coming from just a few countries, it's worth your time to estimate the duties for those countries. Your estimates may have an influence on how you market your products to those countries.

To get general information on duties in other countries, refer to the Country Commercial Guides published by the Department of Commerce. You can get them at *http://www.export.gov/mrllogin.html*. You can add these guides to your trade reference system. Again, your trade reference system can be helpful.

Try the Export Assistance Center at *http://exportassistance.com/ export_education.html* for links to Web resources that include the duties to be paid in various countries. Also refer to the foreign consulates in the US at *http://www.state.gov/s/cpr/rls/fco* for offices perhaps near you for information on duties in foreign countries.

## Couriers

Go to the FedEx Global Trade Manager (*https://gtm.fedex.com/cgi-bin/ doc_det*) where you can calculate online the taxes and duties to be paid. FedEx is still building its global website, and it doesn't cover all countries yet. Nonetheless, it's a convenient resource and a calculator that covers numerous countries. This is the easy way to do it.

UPS also provides similar Web calculations at its Global Advisor, *http:/ /ups.com/globaladvisor*. See Chapter 20 for more about the couriers.

# Effect on Marketing

Chapter 10 pointed out for sales tax, VAT, and excise tax that such taxes can have an effect on how you market your products in certain countries. Duties are no different. They can be small or large percentages, and they can have an effect too.

For instance, if you think that your eBay customer in another country is going to pay the $39.95 discount price that customers in the US pay for an item, your marketing strategy might be X. If you know that there is a 35 percent duty in the country, the item will cost your customers there $53.93; and that's without even figuring VAT or sales tax! It seems to us that your marketing strategy might be Y or Z as a result.

In any event, it's always enlightening to know what your customers have to pay to acquire what you sell.

For a list of the range of duties in global countries (as well as VAT and sales tax), go to:

United States Council for International Business (*http:// www.uscib.org/index.asp?documentID=1676*)

# Summary

The toughest part of calculating duties is classification. That's standardized with an HS six-digit code that works in 176 countries. Once classified properly, it's easy to calculate the duty on an item. Perhaps the easiest way to calculate the duty for an item is to use one of the online calculators offered by one of the couriers.

# *12*

## *Means of Payment*

If you conduct eBay business abroad, the means of payment are more risky than in the US. Certainly payments in the US have their problems, but we hope only occasionally. Payments abroad are even less secure, and you're bound to have more problems, unless you strive for safety. That means safety not only for yourself but for the other party too, whether that party is a buyer or a supplier. Let's take a look at some of the factors to keep in mind and at the different types of payments for goods.

### *Other Chapters*

Note this topic is so important that this book covers it beyond this chapter. Chapter 14 covers letters of credit, a traditional means of payment for import-export. Chapter 15 covers currency exchange, which may have an effect on payment. And Chapters 17-19 cover PayPal, which offers the promise of streamlining global commerce for consumers and small businesses.

# Seller's Concerns

A seller simply wants to get paid for the goods sold. However, in addition, a seller wants to make sure that the buyer is satisfied and protected. Repeat business is easier to get than new business.

## *Payment*

A seller wants to get paid. In a consumer sale, the buyer pays in advance, and this lessens the seller's risk, although there is always the risk of a charge-back should the buyer pay by credit card.

Most eBay businesses will not find themselves in the business of exporting in bulk to another party. If they export in bulk, it will be to a warehouse (i.e., no payment to be collected until subsequent consumer sales are made) or to a joint venturer who is essentially a partner.

The relationship with joint venturers can be almost anything from an importer with whom you do recurring business—thus just another buyer—to someone that has an ownership in your business or in a joint venture. For the former, you need to be careful about collecting payments. For the latter, the financial arrangements are in-house. Depending on the joint-venture arrangement, you might have a hybrid situation.

## Delivery

A seller needs to deliver the goods. That is, a seller has more concern about delivery abroad than domestically because often the transportation distances are greater with a greater likelihood of multiple carriers. If the goods are not delivered, the seller is likely to absorb the loss in eBay consumer transactions—remember the feedback system? That is, the seller won't get paid. In non-consumer transactions, the seller is also unlikely to get paid.

The goods have to arrive undamaged in a timely manner. Damaged goods, goods that arrive two months late, or disappearing (stolen) goods may affect a seller's receipt of payment.

## Receipt

Ship and forget is not a reliable option globally. It may work domestically, although many eBay sellers prudently obtain proof of receipt routinely for domestic sales. For sales abroad proof of delivery is essential due to the additional risk of doing business at long distances with buyers in other countries. This is not a problem as couriers and most carriers have an efficient tracking system for packages which requires a receipt upon delivery.

## Unknown Risks

Sellers should be concerned with unforeseen risks. When the goods get to the other country, will customs let them through? Perhaps they are illegal imports there. Perhaps they are subject to an import quota. Perhaps the duties will be much higher than estimated. Perhaps they will be stolen. These are all concerns that affect delivery, and if the goods aren't delivered, the seller may not get paid.

## Insurance

Insurance can take some of the risk out of a sale abroad, particularly for transportation. Who pays for the insurance? Should a seller require that the delivery be insured? What about the situations that the insurance doesn't cover?

## Currency

The exchange rates normally don't change fast enough to worry about losses suffered due to the decline of the dollar over short periods of time (although at the time the book went to press in 2004 the dollar had been declining steadily for two years). But what happens when delivery takes two months and there is a significant difference in the currency exchange rate? If the purchase wasn't prepaid, who takes the risk of the change in the rate? This is particularly of concern to a US seller when the buyer pays in a foreign currency and the US Dollar is declining. Certainly it would be of concern to a buyer paying in her own country's currency when the US Dollar is rising.

# Buyer's Concerns

A buyer is simply concerned about receiving goods of the quality and in the amount specified in the purchase order.

## Receipt of Goods

The buyer orders specified goods of specified quality and is concerned that such goods arrive as ordered and undamaged. The goods must also arrive in a timely manner.

## Payment

A buyer is naturally hesitant to prepay for orders abroad because of the additional risks in transportation, customs clearance, and obtaining a remedy for a breach of contract. A buyer would rather pay after the receipt of the goods.

## *Unknown Risks*

With courier transportation, the loss and damage risks are minimized. One company handles the packages from the beginning of the journey to the end. But the same is not true with surface transportation.

In addition, the seller prepares the paperwork for customs clearance, but the buyer (or agent) has to do the actual clearance. If there are problems with clearance, it could cost the buyer an unknown extra amount.

### *Courier Subcontractors*

Couriers abroad and even domestically sometimes use subcontractors to deliver packages. Consequently, such packages are probably not as secure as packages handled only by courier employees.

## *Insurance*

Insurance is the key to providing protection against loss for shipping. But other procedures must be employed for protection against malfeasant sellers.

## *Currency*

Currency usually does not pose a problem in the short run. However, it is not unusual for buyers to order goods from a factory. From the time of the order, the manufacturing process and the shipping together could easily take two months or more. During that time the currency exchange rates might change enough to reduce profits significantly.

# Types of Payment

The standard types of payments, not including PayPal, are covered below. This book covers PayPal in Chapters 17-19.

## *Advance Payment*

Advanced payment is the most risky for a buyer. In effect, the buyer accepts the risk of shipping and customs clearance as well as the risk of a seller that does not perform or that doesn't perform according to the purchase order.

### *Cash*

Cash is not a safe way to pay either domestically or abroad.

### *Wire*

Sending the payment amount by bank wire transfer is the traditional way to pay in advance abroad. This can be done from almost any US bank branch if payment is in US Dollars. If the payment needs to be converted into the currency of the seller's country, that's an extra step that some bank branches may not be able to handle.

You can also wire money through Western Union (*http://www.westernunion.com*) almost anywhere in the world. This is primarily limited to consumer transactions and is expensive.

### *Credit Card*

Paying by credit card is a great way to pay. If there is a problem with the seller's performance, you may be able to do a charge-back. And with high credit limits, reasonably large payments are feasible. Keep in mind, however, that first, the seller has to accept credit payment. Second, a charge-back strategy may not give you the protection you need. In a dispute between buyer and seller, it's sometimes difficult to predict who will win in the eyes of the credit card company or bank.

### *Personal (or Business) Check*

Personal (or business) checks are widely accepted and widely used. Why would a seller abroad accept your personal check? Simple. The seller will wait until the check clears before shipping the goods. This may cause undesirable delays.

### Cashier's Check

The cashier's check in the US is often treated like cash. Abroad they are more likely to be treated like personal (or business) checks. A foreign draft is perhaps a more acceptable type of payment abroad. However, you may not be able to get a foreign draft at a branch bank (i.e., only at the main branch).

### Money Order

A money order is like a cashier's check. However, there are exceptions. International money orders, postal money orders, and Western Union money orders may be treated like cash because many people abroad are familiar with them.

You can send money orders from your computer. The post office and Western Union—and perhaps your bank—enable you to purchase and send money orders online. Western Union bought BidPay.com and now calls it Western Union Auction Payments (*http://www.auctionpayments.com*). Many people use money orders like others use checks or credit cards. This is particularly true abroad.

### PayPal

Chapters 17-19 cover PayPal, which is now in over 38 countries. It can be a very convenient, secure, and inexpensive means of payment abroad.

## Letter of Credit

A letter of credit is like a contingent check that pays only on the meeting of certain conditions. Letters of credit are widely used in global commerce. Chapter 13 covers letters of credit.

## Documentary Collection

A documentary collection is like a letter of credit and is covered briefly in Chapter 13.

## Credit

Does credit work abroad? That is, will a seller give you 30-day or 60-day credit? Sure. It's just a matter of trust. If you build a good business relationship with a seller, the seller may provide you with credit to stock your inventory.

## Bank Visits

Note that some of the means of payment such as wire transfers, cashier's checks, foreign drafts, money orders, and letters of credit require a bank visit. That can be a brain-deadening experience that sucks time out of your day. You are better off using a means of payment that you can use in your office without a visit to the bank.

## UPS

United Parcel Service (UPS) offers a list of financial services (*http://www.ups.com/content/corp/bussol/supply/finances.html*) some of which may help you make payments internationally. However, such services offered by UPS and its competitors are aimed at medium to large corporations, and it may not be realistic for small businesses to take advantage of them. Nonetheless, it might be worthwhile for you to review such services occasionally to see what you can use cost-effectively.

## Services

There many global services available that will assist you make payments and other financial arrangements. An example is Commonwealth Foreign Exchange. Visit it at *http://www.comfex.com*.

# Beyond the Sales Price

The sales price is not the only cost of importing goods from abroad. There are other expenses to be paid. They are likely to be paid by a different means than the sales price. So, they are worth mentioning here briefly even though Chapter 15 covers them too.

## Shipping

Shipping abroad is a major expense and likely to be more expensive for consumer goods than shipping inside the US. Who pays? The buyer or seller? And how?

## Insurance

For inexpensive consumer items in the US, sellers can self-insure, buy insurance, or pass the cost of insurance on to the buyer. For more expensive items, insurance should be definitely be obtained. For shipments abroad, however, insurance is a must. Who pays for it and how?

## Duties and Other Taxes

Chapters 10 and 11 outline taxes and duties that may have to be paid on imports. How will these be paid, and by whom?

## Fees

Don't forget freight forwarders and custom brokers charge fees. How do these get paid, and who pays?

# Summary

Many of the normal means of payment work internationally as well as in the US. But some don't work as well and may result in delays (e.g., clearing checks between banks in different countries). For contingent payments, the letter of credit is useful and traditional.

# *13*

## *Letters of Credit*

Letters of credit are a traditional means of making payment for goods bought abroad and shipped to the US for import. They can also be used for exports. These legal instruments (documents) are created by banks (particularly international banks) and handled by banks. The banks provide a valuable service in managing these financial arrangements between the parties. Keep in mind, though, that banks don't provide such services for free. Using letters of credit is another expense of doing business in the import-export world.

# Letter of Credit

Think of a letter of credit as a check with a contingency. That is, it's like a check signed and delivered to the beneficiary (person receiving the money – the seller) but is contingent on the beneficiary doing something (fulfilling certain requirements) in order to be able to cash the check.

## Contingent Check?

But you say, "That's crazy. There's no such thing as a check with a contingency." But that's the point. You need a check with a contingency, but there's no such thing. Consequently, you need a different legal instrument (document) that does what you would want a check with a contingency to do if there were such a thing. That legal instrument is a *letter of credit*.

A letter of credit written by the buyer's bank is delivered to the seller's bank. It states that the buyer's bank will transfer a certain amount of money to the seller's account in the seller's bank if the seller does something specifically required by the buyer (e.g., ships the goods to be imported by the buyer).

### Complex Procedure

Banks handle letters of credit as part of a complex procedure that is over simplified in this chapter for the sake of quick understanding.

## Credit?

What does the word "credit" mean in letter of credit? You can look at this two ways.

From the seller's point of view, the way to look at it is that the letter of credit will credit the seller's bank account with a certain amount of money sometime in the future upon the seller fulfilling certain requirements. It is the obligation of the buyer's bank to make the payment so long as the seller fulfills the requirements.

Let's say you go to First Duluth City Bank (Duluth Bank), to issue a letter of credit to the seller through the seller's bank in India, Chennai Metropolitan Bank (Chennai Bank), for $10,000 to pay for 2,000 cotton Madras shirts you are going to import to the US. At some point in the future (e.g., when the seller ships the shirts), the Duluth Bank will have an obligation to transfer $10,000 into the seller's account at the Chennai Bank in India.

The traditional way to look at the word "credit" from the seller's point of view is that the seller can rely upon the credit of the buyer's bank rather upon the credit of the buyer. That is, so long as the buyer's bank is solvent, the seller knows he will get paid.

### Not All Banks

Not all banks issue letters of credit. In fact, many banks that do issue letters of credit don't do it by themselves. They do it through a major bank with international branches and affiliations. Consequently, if you buy goods in bulk abroad routinely, you may find it advantageous to bank with one of the large international banks to get import-export services directly. Try HSBC (and affiliate banks) at *http://www.hsbc.com*.

Although the Duluth Bank and the Chennai Bank are ficticious examples, it makes sense that a bank in Duluth, a Great Lakes port city (via the St. Lawrence Seaway) in Minnesota, might be a bank you would expect to be involved in international trade.

## Flexible Arrangements

A letter of credit is not like a check, however, in a very important sense. A check is primarily a straightforward and uniform legal instrument for making payments. It's a form to fill out.

From the both the buyer's and seller's points of view, a letter of credit is a more flexible legal instrument. It can have all types of simple or complex contingencies. Although normally irrevocable, it can even be revocable or have other attributes beyond the scope of this chapter. It can be one page or several. It can be custom drafted to fit the situation, or it can be like a form. There's even such a document as a stand-by letter of credit

## *Buyer and Banker*

In other words, using a letter of credit is not like taking out your check book, scribbling a few words and numbers, and thereby making payment. It's something you need to arrange with a bank that handles letters of credit. The bank has to issue the letter of credit and then administer it. For instance, the bank has to determine that all the requirements have been met by the seller before payment will be made. The seller's bank usually gets involved in the process too. Consequently, it's a hands-on type of payment process for the banks involved; that is, it's labor-intensive, which means that it has a significant cost.

## *Funding*

From the buyer's point of view, the funding for the letter of credit can be supported by almost any payment or borrowing arrangement the buyer can make with the issuing bank.

Let's say that the seller will not be able to manufacture and ship the shirts for 90 days. Thus, you have no obligation to make the payment for three months. But the seller wants a letter of credit now. What arrangements will you have to make with the Duluth Bank to support the bank's obligation to pay the seller under the letter of credit 90 days in the future? Keep in mind that once the letter of credit is issued, the Duluth Bank has an obligation to pay the $10,000 so long as your requirements are fulfilled by the seller.

As you can understand, you will have to fund the letter of credit with cash or with whatever credit arrangement you can establish with the bank.

## Cost

What is the cost? Well, that depends on who drafts the letter of credit, who administers it, and how complex the deal is. For transactions under $10,000 US, letters of credit may not be cost effective.

# Purpose

The letter of credit is a traditional means of payment for import-export. You can understand why. It protects both the buyer and seller at the same time. The seller has an obligation to deliver at a certain time and place. The buyer has an obligation to pay a certain amount. When both of these obligation are fulfilled—but not until—the money changes hands. It's similar to putting the transaction into escrow.

# Paperwork

The contingency for a letter of credit is met with paperwork. The list below includes some examples of documents that may be required:

- Commercial invoice (see Chapter 6)
- Bill of lading, a receipt for the goods issued by a carrier
- Warranty of title, by the seller to the buyer regarding the goods
- Letter of indemnity, from the seller to the buyer regarding certain stated circumstances

Depending on the sales contract, bank requirements, and situational requirements, a number of different documents might be required.

In our example, the seller presents the documents representing 2,000 Madras shirts to the seller's bank, the Chennai Bank. The Chennai

Bank in India then assembles the documents together with the letter of credit from the Duluth Bank and examines them to make sure they meet all the contingencies. The Chennai Bank then sends them to the Duluth Bank for payment. The Duluth Bank receives the documents and examines them to make sure they meet all the contingencies. The Duluth Bank then wires the Chennai Bank $10,000 for deposit in the sellers account. The Duluth Bank gives the documents to the buyer. This is a simplification of what happens, but you get the idea.

### Documents

Although the transaction in regard to a letter of credit is contingent on delivery of the goods, the goods are represented by documents. Consequently, the contingency is met by delivery of the appropriate paperwork (i.e., documents that show unambiguously that the goods were delivered). *Therefore, it is extremely important that the documents agree with the sales contract and otherwise be accurate and complete.*

However, don't get the mistaken notion that the paperwork is all that's important. The documents represent actual specific events such as the delivery of the goods to a specific place at a certain time.

Note that the transportation and delivery point can be anywhere the parties agree. See Chapter 21 for some standard arrangements defined by Incoterms 2000.

For a more in-depth understanding of letters of credit read *http:// crfonline.org/orc/cro/cro-9-1.html* and *http://crfonline.org/orc/cro-9-2.html*. The International Chamber of Commerce publishes standard rules for letters of credit in *Uniform Customs and Practice for Documentary Credits* (UCP 500), *http://www.iccwbo.org/home/statements_rules/ statements/2003/banking_documents.asp.*

## *Online*

To initiate letters of credit online, consult with a bank that provides international banking services. For instance, visit the Wells Fargo Bank website at *http://www.wellsfargo.com/com/ceo/ilc.jhtml* where you can initiate a letter of credit (requires an existing banking relationship with Wells Fargo). Some other banks also enable the initiation of letters of credit online for their customers, a practice that will help make these arrangements more efficient and less expensive.

Visit Wells Fargo International Services for information on their global commerce services at *http://www.wellsfargo.com/inatl/inatl.jhtml*.

### *Leading Edge?*

There is an online letter-of-credit service that looks interesting for basic situations. Take a look at Secure LC at *http://www.securelc.com*. It is an escrow-letter-of-credit arrangement for a fee of 0.5 percent (e.g., $50 for a $10,000 transaction). Although it doesn't appear to allow for complex letter-of-credit transactions, the price is reasonable. We don't know enough about this company located in Hong Kong to recommend it. So, check it out thoroughly before you use its service.

Is this the leading edge in the import-export business, or is it just another online scheme that won't last? Only time will tell.

# Documentary Collection

A documentary collection arrangement is similar to a letter of credit arrangement in that the buyer's bank and the seller's bank administer the details of the contingency payment. But there is not letter of credit document. Rather it is like a Cash on Delivery (COD) arrangement.

# Coordination

As you will note from reading Chapters 5-9, the seller (exporter) is responsible for the proper documentation for customs clearance and the buyer (importer) is usually responsible for the clearance. (Although, the parties can change the normal way of doing things if they agree to do so.)

When you add a freight forwarder or customs broker to the transaction, everything must be coordinated according to the roles that each party and each service provider plays. For instance, the freight forwarder or customs broker will want to make sure the seller is required to deliver the proper documents in a certain format along with the goods, thus making the clearance process proceed smoothly. The buyer's bank will have its own requirements regarding the paperwork necessary to satisfy the letter of credit. Then too, a freight forwarder, rather than the seller's bank, might be the one to provide the documents to the buyer's bank.

These processes need to be coordinated. Contacting your customs broker or freight forwarder as well as your banker before the sales agreement is finalized will help ensure the transaction is planned properly and is subsequently well coordinated.

# Summary

A letter of credit is a promise of payment by the buyer's bank contingent on the seller delivering the goods at a time in the future. It's a traditional means of payment in the import-export business, and many eBay businesses use it to pay for goods abroad which they import into the US for sale on eBay US. It may not be cost-effective to use it for small payments, but for payments over $10,000 US it's a payment process you may find practical. The interesting question is whether this process can be duplicated by an alternative payment process that's more cost-efficient? See Chapter 19.

# 14

## *Currency Exchange*

Currencies from different countries fluctuate in value compared to each other. That is to say, the money of one country rises and falls in value compared to the money of other countries. For instance, one day a US Dollar may be worth 8 Swedish Kronor. A week later it may be worth 7.75 Kronor. What forces create these curious fluctuations?

Actually, money is much like a commodity. It fluctuates in value like other commodities such as wheat, beef, or copper. Indeed, commodities markets are much like the stock market, always in flux. So, the same forces that create ongoing fluctuations in the stock market also create ongoing fluctuations in currency exchange.

Those forces include the state of a country's economy, productivity, political stability, trade balances, current events, political intentions, industrial trends, and dozens of others. Certainly it is well beyond the scope of this book to document and explain currency fluctuations. Suffice to say such fluctuations always exist.

So long as currency fluctuations are stable—take place within a narrow range of values—the effect on international trade is not a major concern. When fluctuations start a trend, however, the import-export business can become more risky.

For instance, by the spring of 2004 the US Dollar had fallen about 30 percent in value over a two-year period. That meant a US importer at the end of the two-year period had 30 percent less purchasing power in other countries. This trend started after a long period of stability for the US Dollar.

### A Simple Purchase

When you exchange currency, you are simply using a certain amount of dollars to purchase a certain amount of another country's currency.

### Currency Exchange Practicalities

See Chapter 18 for a discussion of the practicalities of currency exchanges in eBay transactions. This chapter deals primarily in currency exchange issues for bulk purchases.

# Dealing with Fluctuations

The exchange rate between two currencies depends on two countries. A country may experience circumstances that increase the value of its currency, and the exchange rate becomes more favorable. A country may experience circumstances that decrease the value of its currency, and the exchange rate will become more unfavorable. Each country has its little ups and downs, which occur at the same time as the other country's little ups and downs. Thus, exchange rates are dynamic—always in fluctuation—between countries.

If your profit margin is two percent or if your imports or exports are worth a huge amount of money, even normal currency fluctuations can be risky for you. You will have to develop a strategy to time your transactions precisely and get your risk under control. It might be that the import-export business isn't feasible (profitable) for you.

If you have a high profit margin or your imports or exports are not huge, you have less to worry about. Nonetheless, discipline in timing your purchases of foreign currency will help minimize the impact of surprises in the exchange rates when they occur.

## Timing

Suppose you decide to import 100 bicycles into the US from South Korean for 14,400,000 Won. The exchange value is $12,000 at the time the purchase agreement is made. After your cost of goods and total expenses are figured, you expect to make a profit of 10 percent selling the bicycles on eBay US.

In order to understand this transaction, we have to analyze it further.

**$12,000 Cost of Goods** This is the cost of the imported bicycles as if the currency exchange were made on the same day as the purchase agreement.

**$15,450 Total Expenses** This is all your expenses including normal overhead, payment to employees or independent contractors, shipping, import duties and the like. It also includes payment to yourself.

**$30,500 Sales** You expect to sell the bikes on eBay for an average of $305 each.

**$3,050 Profit** This is your 10 percent profit.

## Profit

What is profit? For most small businesses, profit is simply what's left over after all the cost of goods and expenses are paid. In this case, there is $3,050 left over. But let's explore this a little further. When you're in business for yourself, your expenses don't include what you pay yourself. Suppose you had allocated $7,450 of your annual payment to yourself to this transaction. In this case, the $7,450 (that portion of your annual payment to yourself allocated to this transaction in your business) plus $3,050 (the 10 percent profit) equals $10,500 your total profit for this transaction. This is 34 percent of the transaction. That is, your profit is really 34 percent because your business is personally owned, operated, and managed.

Investors are needed for many businesses, however, and investors look for a return on their money. Suppose you have investors in the business. The profit then becomes the lower figure of 10 percent. After all, someone has to operate and manage the business (that's you), and managers typically get paid before investors (e.g., the managers and employees of a company get paid before the stockholders). Therefore, with investors involved, that portion of your annual payment to yourself that you allocate to this transaction ($7,450) is really an expense, not part of the profit. It's part of your salary.

Why go to the trouble to make this distinction between sole ownership and ownership with an investors involved in a book on eBay import-export? We do this simply to show the potential effect of currency exchange on your business.

### Bank Loan

Keep in mind that if you borrow money from a bank, the bank is a major investor in your business. The 10 percent profit goes to cover the debt service (loan payments) on the loan.

## *Example*

Suppose you make a contract to pay for the 100 South Korean bicycles in 35 days from the date of contract at the time manufacture will be completed and the bikes will be immediately shipped to the US. Subsequently, during that 35 days, the value of the US dollar sinks 5 percent against the Won.

The $12,000 you must pay for your cost of goods has increased 5 percent ($600) due to the change in the exchange rate. It's now $12,600. Assuming you can't increase your sales revenue, your profit has declined $600.

If you operate your company as a personal business without investors, your profit of $10,250 declines to $9,650 (an 6 percent decline). This is not disastrous, but it's a situation you would rather avoid.

If you have investors involved in your business, your profit goes from $3,050 to $2,450 (a 20 percent decline). This has the potential for being disastrous. If investors do not make a return on their investment, they will start to think about ways to get out. A 20 percent decline in their return on investment will not create a happy situation.

OK, you can tell your investors that they won't really experience a 20 percent decline in profit because you're going to make it up out of the $7,450 of your annual payment to yourself that you allocated to this transaction. But this is your salary. Are you going to make up every shortfall in business out of your salary just to keep investors happy? As a practical matter, you may have to do so from time to time, but it's not a good business practice.

### *Bank*

If a bank has loaned you money, the resulting funds after the

decline in profit ($2,450) may not be enough to cover the debt ser-
vice. This will start to get you in trouble with the bank unless you
cover the decline in profit out of your salary.

---

## Conclusion

As you will conclude from our example, an unfavorable change in the
exchange rate has the potential to bleed your profits dry. You have to
manage the exchange situation closely in order to preserve the profit
in the transaction.

## Risk

When you agree today to pay in a foreign currency for an import at
some point in the future and you do not buy the currency today, you
run the risk of the currency exchange becoming unfavorable in the
future. The question is, "Should you bear that risk alone?" That certainly is a point of negotiation in any purchase agreement. Who will
bear the risk of exchange rate fluctuations?

Certainly, if your agreement requires you to make payment in dollars,
there is no risk to you. The other party takes all the risk. As a practical
matter, you might want to negotiate an agreement in which both parties bear some of the risk.

## Responsibility

Fluctuations in currency exchanges can be a harsh risk. Sometimes
currencies can be stable for a long time. Businesspeople come to take
stability for granted. Then suddenly in a short time exchange rates can
change dramatically with a potentially cataclysmic effect on import-
export business. Unfortunately, there is no high authority to which to
appeal. If you have not prepared to minimize your risk, your profit
and perhaps even your business is at risk.

In other words, it's your responsibility to prepare for the harsh realities
of currency exchange. What can you do? Here are some ideas:

1.  Pay in dollars rather than another currency.

2.  Buy the foreign currency at the time of the agreement rather than wait until payment is required.

3.  Keep a dollar reserve specifically to purchase the foreign currency needed just as soon as the exchange rate starts to move in an unfavorable direction.

4.  Hedge by purchasing currency buy options (read below).

5.  Include in your agreement with the other party a provision that shares the risk of currency exchange rate fluctuations.

## Hedging

There is a way to create insurance, in effect, that will preserve your profit even if you get stuck with an ill-timed and unfavorable change in the exchange rate. You simply purchase a currency option. In this case, you want an option that will become more valuable as the exchange becomes more unfavorable. Thus, your decline in profit will be compensated (nullified) by an increase in the value of the option.

For this purpose, you will need a buy option ("call" in Wall Street terminology) or "forward contract." You pay a small price to buy the right from someone to buy from them the currency at the original exchange rate even when the value of the US Dollar decreases. That is, they are obligated to sell you the currency at the option price regardless of what the market price is when the option is exercised.

Suppose you buy an option for $1 to buy from someone the amount of 1,200 Won for $100. The exchange declines 5 percent. Now $100 is worth only 1,140 Won. But the right to buy 1,200 Won for $100 is now worth $5 because you can exercise the option and make $5. The cost to you is the original $1 that you paid (i.e., 1 percent).

### Out of a Pool

You don't buy an option from a specific person. You buy it out of a pool of options that numerous people have created.

If this seems complicated, just understand that you buy a security (call option) that goes up in value as the exchange rate becomes more unfavorable. Were the exchange rate to become favorable, the call option would diminish in value until it was worth next to nothing. Your cost for this insurance is simply the price of the option.

This scheme is called hedging and is widespread in business, especially for businesses that have well-recognized uncertainties. Indeed, hedging is commonly used in import-export for currency exchange.

To go to the trouble of hedging, you have to have a sizable amount of potential currency exchange at stake. But it's like anything else. Once you learn to do it efficiently, it will work well for smaller amounts too and will bring more stability to your import-export business.

# Exchanging Currency

Where do currency exchanges take place? Many financial institutions, organizations, and governments operate currency exchanges. The only one you need be concerned with is the one you use. That is likely to be the exchange your bank (or an affiliated financial institution) operates. But special services such as Commonwealth Foreign Exchange (*http://www.comfex.com*) are worth exploring.

### Cost

Exchanges are not done for free. There is a fee. Naturally, your objective as a good businessperson is to find the lowest fee charged and do your exchange business with that financial institution. As a practical matter, however, you will probably exchange currency via your own bank, assuming the rate is reasonable.

# Banks

Banks usually charge reasonable fees for currency exchanges and make it easy to do an exchange. Most other exchange operations charge higher fees. Your objective is to find an exchange operation less expensive than your bank—if you can. Check the rates that your bank charges and compare them to other exchange operations. The differences may not be worth losing any sleep over, but you won't know until you compare.

---

### What Bank?

If you are going to do import-export business, you need a bank that provides adequate import-export financial services. If you live in rural Wyoming, you will probably not find such a bank close by. Nonetheless, there plenty of inland cities that have banks with import-export experience. Air cargo has made every city with a jet-port a potential international port city. Import-export is no longer just the province of seaport cities.

What you would like to avoid, if possible, is a bank that provides you with import-export services through another bank and charges a mark-up on the normal fees.

---

## Timing

What this chapter is all about is timing. If you make an agreement today to pay 14,400,000 Won (that you can buy today for $12,000) for 100 bicycles and you buy that Won today, currency exchange is irrelevant. However, if you don't have to make payment for 60 days and you plan to purchase the Won on the 60th day, you are taking the risk that the price of Won may go up significantly during the 60 days.

Indeed, the message of this chapter is simply that when the signing of the agreement and the payment do not coincide, you need to act to minimize your risk.

# Currency Restrictions

Currency exchange rates are determined by the marketplace; that is, except when they're determined by a government. The dynamics of currency exchange rates are complex and beyond the scope of this book. You should be aware, however, that some countries do regulate currency exchange rates. In addition, some countries regulate payments either coming into the country, going out of the country, or both. Moreover, many countries have restrictions in regard to the amounts of money that can cross borders. You may run into these restrictions in your import-export activities, and you want to make sure you comply with them, keeping in mind that each country is different.

# Summary

For many eBay businesses that do not deal in bulk purchases or bulk sales abroad, this chapter is much ado about nothing. Otherwise, currency exchange is a factor that you will want to plug into your financial equations.

# *15*

## *Operational Costs*

So far we've been talking about a lot of things that cost money. In subsequent chapters we will be talking about more things. And they all add up. Sometimes the seller pays them. Sometimes the buyer pays them. You need to keep track of them. They affect your operating costs. Duties, sales taxes, VATs, excise taxes, brokers and agents fees, bank fees, currency exchange fees, and the like need to be accounted for in regard to each product. The first step is to take an inventory of them. The next step is to account for them product by product.

# Survey of Costs

The following is a sample survey of the costs you may incur in the operation of your global business via eBay. There will be products that may have additional costs due to certain regulations.

## Trade Reference System

A trade reference system, while necessary, doesn't have to be expensive. In fact, potentially it can be just a list of Web links. Still, someone has to take the time and energy to put it together and keep it current. If you buy publications for it, they will run up your costs for it.

## Document Preparation

If you're well organized, you can use your auction management software to generate the paperwork necessary for doing business abroad. If you do, it shouldn't add much to your overhead.

## Customs Brokers and Freight Forwarder Fees

As a small business you cannot afford to employ full-time personnel to handle customs clearance. If you're an importer, you will need to hire customs brokers or freight forwarders (with customs brokerage departments) to clear products through customs in the US or Canada. If you're an exporter, you will have to do so in other countries. Even large companies use customs brokers and freight forwarders. The only exception to this is low cost items sent via the post office that can take advantage of the inexpensive customs clearance provided through the post office.

## Sales Taxes, VATs, Excise Taxes, and Duties

These taxes can add up faster than you can say "unprofitable." Remember that the buyer-importer normally pays these. But also remember that you can be the seller and importer at the same time. We have said that taking care of theses taxes and other import costs is great customer service. Thus, should you chose to provide such customer service, you will have to pay these.

## Bank Fees

There are bank fees for foreign drafts, wire transfers, letters of credit, cashier's checks, and the like. The banks will nickel and dime you to death if you're not careful.

## Currency Exchange Fees

When you exchange currency, there's always a fee paid. Usually it's paid to the bank. If the other party offers to exchange currency for you, they will charge you a fee or pass along the bank fee to you (in the exchange rate). Even PayPal charges a fee for exchanging currency.

## Escrow Fees

If you should decide to use an escrow arrangement rather than a letter of credit, you will pay an escrow fee. Letters of credit are used more than escrow for deals abroad, but if you can find a legitimate international escrow company, you might try it, particularly if it's less expensive than a letter of credit.

## Special Packaging

Will you have to package an item for extra durability? Perhaps not for the couriers. You can check courier packaging requirements at their websites. But for surface shipping or for the post office, assume that a package will go through harsher treatment than it will in the US or Canada. Again, check the post office websites for packaging requirements.

## Shipping

Shipping is a bigger expense for transactions abroad than in the US or Canada. You need to accurately estimate the cost of shipping to see how it fits into your overall sales scheme. If you're a buyer, it is a significant cost of purchase.

## Insurance

Insurance is more necessary for commerce abroad than domestically, and you will want to make sure your items are insured for shipping.

## Communications

You can't do it all with email. Sometimes you have to pick up the phone and dial to negotiate or to get things straightened out. Long distance phone calls abroad can get expensive.

## Travel

There are two sides to this topic. You may have to visit countries abroad in order to make your business successful. On the other hand, you may want to visit other countries and use your eBay import-export business to write off the travel expenses. Either way, travel becomes a significant cost.

## Warehousing

The cost of warehousing can become significant. The longer the goods are stored, the greater the expense. Bonded warehousing used for interim storage in the customs procedure adds to the cost of clearing customs. But not many eBay businesses will use bonded warehousing. Many will use cross-border warehousing, a significant expense. And cross-border warehousing can actually save you money when you provide customs clearance for your customers (buyers) as part of your customer service.

## Additional Administration

There is no doubt that buying and selling abroad takes an extra measure of administration in your business. That will cost you extra money or time.

# Accounting

Accurate accounting of your import-export costs enables you to analyze your eBay business activities to answer two questions. Is an imported or exported product adequately profitable? Is the eBay import-export business itself profitable?

## *Product Profitability*

*eBay Business the Smart Way* discusses the product profit model. It shows the cost of selling a product with a portion of general overhead included in the cost figures. You use it to discover the profitability of selling a particular product and then make a judgement as to whether the profit is enough for you. For global sales this analysis is valid, too, but your costs will be higher.

## *Business Profitability*

After all is said and done, it's the total profit of your business that matters. The products must be profitable, and combined they must add up to a profitable business. Otherwise, what's the point? The sales you make abroad will have additional costs and will affect your overall bottom line.

# Summary

When you sell, there are certain costs the buyer covers. As we discussed before, you need to know those costs. Knowing what the total cost of a product is to a consumer will give you a clearer picture of whether sales abroad are feasible or can be expanded. This information may affect the way you market your product to consumers abroad.

Of course, when you pay the costs, as a seller, you have to know what they will be for the purposes of planning. Then you have to carefully account for them. If you don't, you won't know whether you're going to make a profit. Then you will have to recoup the costs through charging a shipping and handling fee or by setting a higher price.

# *16*

## *Fraud*

It's tough to write a book or a chapter on eBay fraud. Just when you cover one scam, it's old news and a new one pops up. Con artists are clever people. They can fool even the most careful of us honest folks. What can you do to keep from being a victim? The answer is to use common sense and don't take undue risks. And don't deal with dishonest people.

That's easy to say but difficult to do. eBay is a friendly place where you can trust the vast majority of buyers and sellers. The fraud rate is quite low. Yet you must tailor your actions and communications to protect yourself from a few bad actors. It makes for schizophrenic behavior on your part, being nice one minute and demanding authentication the next. But that's what good business people do in the normal course of business. Until you have dealt with another party several times, you have only a thin basis on which to trust them.

Fortunately, eBay makes it easier to trust someone by operating the feedback system. It works surprisingly well, although it's not 100 percent foolproof.

Of course, what makes eBay US susceptible to fraud is geographical diversity. It's tough to chase a con artist in Maine when you live in Missouri. This impracticality is accentuated globally. In the US, practical remedies for fraud are few and far between. Abroad they are, for all practical purposes, non-existent.

# Follow the Rules

As you read about eBay scams, you get the impression that a fair number of the successful scams entice victims to break some eBay rule or neglect an eBay safeguard.

For instance, many scams start with eBay but are conducted off eBay. Once you're off eBay, you have none of the eBay protections including the capability to leave feedback to warn other eBay members. (Remember that other eBay members before you may have been victims of the same scam but could not leave feedback to warn you because the scam took place off eBay.) Immediately suspect anyone of being dishonest who suggests that you conduct a transaction off eBay, particularly when such conduct is in violation of eBay rules.

### Off-eBay Transactions

Many off-eBay transactions are legitimate. For instance, suppose a potential buyer contacts you after you've auctioned off a new 120 GB hard drive; that is, after the auction is complete. You are not

running another auction for a 120 GB hard drive. The buyer asks if
you have any more to sell. That's legit. But it's off eBay.

Always check the other party's feedback. If their feedback is questionable, don't do business with them. If they have no feedback, be cautious. If you do a transaction off eBay, you may not even know the other party's eBay ID to be able to check their feedback or to even be able to check whether the person is an eBay member. In that case, you're completely on your own.

### Verification

Verifying people and addresses is just a matter of eBay or PayPal checking a person's information via credit card systems or credit agency databases. For instance, let's say  you're doing business with Deborah T. Wilson residing at 533 Ocean Way, Ormond Beach, Florida. If eBay or PayPal compares that information to Deborah's credit card or the the database of one of the big three credit agencies and the information is the same, it's verified. The chances are pretty good that Deborah is a real person with a real address. If the information doesn't match or there is no Deborah T. Wilson on record, then eBay or PayPal will not mark her as verified.

eBay and PayPal do more thorough verifications for certain members who sell expensive items or a high volume of items. But this is an abritrary program, and the members thus verified are not designated as being verified to a higher degree.

Keep in mind, however, that verification is not foolproof. It would take a lot more time, effort, and investigation to produce a near foolproof verification.

Indeed, eventually it is likely that everyone online who wants to be taken seriously in commerce or otherwise will have to undergo a rigorous verification so that there is little doubt that they are who they say they are. If you know who someone is and where they live, you have a better chance of pursuing them for fraud. Someday when eBay matures and stops growing at a high rate, it will probably takes additional steps to make its huge marketplace more secure, and strict verification is likely to be one of the reforms, particularly for transactions of high monetary value. But such a level of verification is not required today.

# Take Precautions

Taking precautions is the best way to prevent fraud. Following sound practices will reduce your risk.

## Check the Feedback

The genius of eBay is the feedback system. Don't be a fool. Use it. Check the other party's feedback. Duh!

We continue to be amazed at the number of people who didn't check the other party's feedback and became victims of fraud. Checking feedback is not foolproof, but it works amazingly well.

Analyze the feedback. If the seller in Japan has 80 transactions, all with positive feedback, is she a good risk? You look at the feedback and find she has made 80 purchases at an average of $6 each. But now she wants to sell a $50,000 Lexus with 4,000 miles on it for $25,000 to be delivered in the US. Is this your next car? Or, is this the dumbest thing you will ever do?

## Countries

According to an MSNBC article, April 1, 2004, the highest risk countries for online fraud are:

Yugoslavia

Nigeria

Romania

Pakistan

Indonesia

Macedonia

Bulgaria

Ukraine

Lebanon

Lithuania

Source: Merchant Risk Council

Other organizations have made other lists of bad guys, and you might consider banning sales to countries on this list or on other such lists. But the truth is that just being careful is your first line of defense.

## Disputes

Disputes aren't fraud, but sometimes they are just as painful. Use a dispute resolution service such as SquareTrade, *http://www.square-trade.com*, to help you resolve disputed issues with another party.

# Sellers Take Precautions

A brief review of a few preventative practices on your part will minimize your risk of fraud.

## It's the Address

It's the address that makes the difference. If a buyer's address is confirmed, they are more likely to be legitimate than if their address is not confirmed. Why? A con artist doesn't want his victims to know where he lives. Make sure the buyer has a confirmed address. If not, ask the buyer to get it confirmed. The corollary guideline to this for sellers is, never ship to an address other than the confirmed address of the buyer. And never ship to a post office box. Unfortunately, as this book went to press, eBay offered confirmed addresses for only the US, Canada, and the United Kingdom.

For PayPal, ship only to the country where the buyer's PayPal account is held. You can find this with the buyer's PayPal address. Also, the shipment must be to a country where PayPal's has memberships. The countries are listed in Chapter 18.

## Commodity Sales

Selling popular commodity big-ticket items abroad are riskier sales than other expensive items, because such items are easy to resell. They include cameras, DVD players, electronics, jewelry, computers, and the like.

## Proof of Delivery

Proof of deliver from the shipper is important for domestic sales. It's particularly important for international shipments. It's just another precaution that prevents fraud. Tracking and proof of delivery is a common service for the couriers. It's not for the post office, but you can get it from the post office for an additional cost.

## Multiple Payments

Do not accept payments from multiple credit cards or multiple PayPal accounts to pay for one item.

## Stolen Credit Cards

Stealing credit numbers is a growth industry in many other countries. The numbers can be stolen individually (e.g., in a restaurant) or in bulk (e.g., from an online vendor database). They are then used to order items online. The best way to protect against such fraud is to ship only to the address registered with the credit card company for a particular credit card number. Items ordered on a US credit card number (e.g., with a US name) for delivery abroad are particularly suspect.

One way to avoid credit card fraud is to not accept credit cards. Moreover, you can refuse to accept PayPal accounts funded by credit cards. Accept only PayPal accounts funded by bank accounts. Thus, you cannot become a charge-back victim. Unfortunately, this is not good customer service, as many people want and need to use credit cards.

Stealing credit cards, credit card numbers, and identities is also a problem in the US but not to the same extent as abroad.

# Buyers Take Precautions

Buyers must be just as careful as sellers.

## Big-Ticket Items

Beware of sellers from abroad selling big-ticket items (e.g., automobiles). They may want to put the deal in escrow, ostensibly to protect you. The escrow company, however, can be bogus (i.e., created by the seller). You send your money via cashier's check or wire, and both the seller and the escrow company disappear with your money. You will never see the big-ticket item.

There are legitimate escrow companies you can use (see below). Insist on using one of them if you buy something expensive from someone abroad. Or, insist on other fraud protection for big-ticket items.

## Escrow

Putting a transaction in escrow solves a lot of fraud risks. However, you need to make sure the escrow company itself isn't a fraud. eBay recommends the following:

**Escrow.com**, *https://www.escrow.com*, for eBay US and eBay Canada

**TradeSecure**, *http://www.tradesecure.com.au/ebay/*, for eBay Australia

**Iloxx SafeTrade**, *http://ebay.iloxx.de*, for eBay Germany

**Escrow Europa**, *http://www.escrow-europa.com*, for ebay Italy and eBay Spain

**Triple Deal**, *http://www.tripledeal.com/frames/index2.html*, for eBay France, eBay Netherlands, and eBay Belgium

Be wary of other online escrow companies, and check them out thoroughly at SOS for Auctions, *http://www.sos4auctions.com*.

## Charge-Back

If you use a credit card to purchase and item and you don't get it, charge it back. Contact your credit card company (bank) and inform them that you did not get what you paid for. If the charge-back is not disputed by the seller, the bank will credit your card card account. If the charge-back is disputed, the bank will investigate to determine whether the charge-back is legitimate.

## Buyer Protections Plans

Take advantage of buyer protection plans wherever they are offered. Unfortunately, eBay offers them in the US but hasn't yet expanded them abroad.

# Fraud Information Resources

Review the following websites occasionally to find out about the latest scams and risks and also to find places to report fraud:

**Fraud.org**, *http://www.fraud.org*

**FraudWatch International**, *http://www.fraudwatchinternational.com*

**Scambusters**, *http://scambusters.org*

# IV

## PayPal Finance

# 17

## *PayPal Basics*

Over half the payments made on eBay go through PayPal. That may mean half the sellers or half the buyers on eBay don't use PayPal yet. In any event, it does mean that many buyers and sellers don't use Pay-Pal. So, we will present it in this book starting with the basics, even though many readers are probably using it already. We feel that it's potentially quite important to international transactions. It's simply an easier, quicker, less expensive, and more convenient way of paying than the traditional cashier's check, foreign draft, or wire transfer typically used in global transactions.

Consequently, this chapter presents the basics. Chapter 18 covers the relatively new PayPal international system for payments. Finally, Chapter 19 covers how PayPal might be used in the future to eliminate letters of credit.

Keep in mind that PayPal doesn't have to be used in conjunction with eBay. You can use it for non-eBay transactions too.

# How It Works

Each person has a PayPal account, like a bank account. There are personal accounts, Premier accounts, and business accounts.

## *Receiving Payment*

When someone pays you via PayPal, the funds go into your account. At that point you have three choices:

1. You can transfer the funds from your PayPal account to your bank account.

2. You can use the funds in your PayPal account to make purchases (assuming the recipients accept PayPal).

3. You can leave the funds in your PayPal account and use your account like a bank account.

You can receive funds for no cost so long as the person paying does not use a credit card for PayPal transactions.

If the person paying uses a credit card as a source of funds for her PayPal payments, then the payment to you will be subject to a small percentage charge (about 3 percent). This charge is just PayPal passing along the amount that PayPal has to pay the credit card company plus a small markup.

With your personal PayPal account, you will not be able to accept credit-card-funded PayPal payments. You will have to upgrade to a PayPal Premier or business account to do so.

## Making Payment

Suppose you have no money in your account. How can you make a payment to someone? Well, PayPay requires you to use your bank account or your credit card as a source of funds.

### Bank Account

If you use your bank account as a source of funds, each time you make a PayPal payment (assuming there are no funds in your PayPal account) PayPal will make an instant electronic withdrawal from your bank account. This works seamlessly and requires no action on your part.

### Credit Card

If you use your credit card as a source of funds, each time you make a PayPal payment (assuming there are no funds in your PayPal account) PayPal will make an instant charge to your credit card. This works automatically and requires no action on your part.

### Acquired Funds

When you acquire funds (receive payment) in your PayPal account and do not withdraw the funds, PayPal will use those funds to fund your payments until such funds are completely depleted. Thereafter, it will use your bank account or your credit card to fund payments.

## Receiving a Specific Payment

To get paid for something, you can send a PayPal email to the person who will pay. This is a request for payment. It's just like sending a person a bill or invoice. The PayPal-originated email requests that the person pay by PayPal.

If the person does not have a PayPal account, the email via links to webpages instructs her how to open an account. If she already has a PayPal account, she simply needs to send you a PayPal payment. The funds are transmitted automatically and instantly into your PayPal account, and you are notified by email that payment has been made.

## Making a Specific Payment

To make a payment, you have PayPal transfer funds from your PayPal account into the other person's PayPal account. PayPal sends the other person an email notifying her that the funds have been transferred.

## Email Address

PayPal works with email addresses. You are identified by your email address. The people with whom you do business via PayPal are identified by their email addresses.

## Login

To make and request payments via PayPal you have to log in to the PayPal website. Your login name (ID) is your email address. Thus, your login password is your primary protection against a criminal misusing your account. Make sure you use a random-character password of at least eight characters and protect it (keep it secret).

## Like a Bank

PayPal is like a bank. Your PayPal account is like a bank account. PayPal even keeps records for you that you can access anytime online at the PayPal website.

## Fraud

PayPal claims its fraud rate is 60-70 percent lower than merchant credit card accounts (less than 0.5 percent). This results from PayPal's fraud prevention systems and techniques which include:

- 128-bit encryption (military grade)
- Pre- and post-transaction screening

- Bank account verification

- Credit card verification

- State-of-the-art neural network risk models

- Industry techniques and patent-pending methods

- Fraud prevention team

- Free $500 US buyer protection coverage for eBay purchases (if seller meets requirements) and paid coverage (Money Back Guarantee) available up to $1,000 US.

- Free seller protection policy (if seller meets requirements)

The seller protection policy requires that the seller follow the rules below. The seller must:

- Be a Verified Business or Premier accountholder

- Ship to the buyer's PayPal address

- Ship within seven days of payment

- Provide proof of shipment and receipt

- Ship tangible goods (intangibles including services and digital goods are not covered)

- Accept a single PayPal payment

- Not impose a surcharge for paying by PayPal

- Respond to buyer complaints within seven days

PayPal also offers a special free World Seller Program to sellers who consistently sell a high volume of goods across borders. If you sell a high volume abroad (over $5,000 US in three months), you will want to check this out. (As this book went to press, the World Seller Program applied only to sellers selling to US buyers. However, PayPal is expanding its coverage.)

Buyer-related loss rates (charge-backs) for sellers are 4-6 times lower with PayPal too.

Visit the PayPal Security Center (*https://www.paypal.com/us/cgi-bin/ webscr?cmd=_security-center*) to review all the security information presented there. Such a visit may save you untold dollars in fraud losses. Fraud losses are more likely when selling globally, and you want to make sure you understand the risks you face and preventative measures you can take.

# Verification

People are linked to their bank accounts. You have to have a name and address to get a bank account. People are also tracked by the major credit agencies. The agencies know who you are and where you live. And credit card companies (and banks) can verify people and addresses, a fact that PayPal takes advantage of.

### Not a Credit Check

When a financial institution checks a person and address for verification against the database of a major credit agency, it's not the same as a credit check. It's simply a confirmation that the name and address are real. This is not 100 percent foolproof against fraud, but it prevents a great deal of fraud.

## PayPal Verification

If PayPal can verify that you are a real person with a bank account or credit card, PayPal allows you to use more of its features and programs and at the same time increases the security of other members. Verification is simply a security measure.

## Confirmed Address

A confirmed address is one that has been verified. A confirmation links the name and bank account or credit card together with an address. If you ship to a buyer with a PayPal confirmed address, you know that the item will go to the address of the bank account or credit card holder. This reduces the risk of fraud considerably. In fact, a request by a buyer to ship to a different address than that of the bank account or credit holder may indicate an attempt at fraud. A confirmed address is a higher level of security than a simple verification.

# What and Where?

This chapter is a general explanation of PayPal as it works in the US. Outside the US, many of the PayPal features and programs may not yet be available in the countries where PayPal already offers memberships. PayPal has to clear all its financial programs through local regulatory labyrinths, and it has not yet completed that huge task for all the PayPal membership countries. In addition, the financial and credit institutions PayPal relies on in the US may not exist in other countries or may not provide the same data infrastructure. Check PayPal's local rules (for each country) and local features before planning your market strategy in a country abroad.

The PayPal Help Center (*http://www.paypal.com/cgi-bin/web-scr?cmd=_help-ext&eloc=0&loc=4&source_page=_home&flow=*) is a good place to find out the features and programs for which you qualify or for which your customers qualify.

### A Rocky Road?

To listen the complaints about PayPal in the US, one would think it's a defunct service. The complaints seem legitimate. Because the PayPal features and services internationally are not on a par with PayPal in the US, the complaints pour in from abroad too. Is this a rocky road to ecommerce security?

We don't think so. The PayPal transactions number in the millions. The complaints are from a few. By far the vast majority of PayPal transactions close without adverse incidents. PayPal is not perfect, but it works pretty well.

# Summary

Why are we devoting three chapters to PayPal? Simply put, PayPal is the salvation of global consumer ecommerce. eCommerce is simply not as safe without PayPal. In particular, global ecommerce is not safe without PayPal. Or, to be even more specific, buying or selling on eBay where buyers and sellers are in different countries is not as safe without PayPal. Indeed, were it not for PayPal, the potential for buying and selling abroad would not be enough to justify publishing this book. PayPal is the eBay gateway to success internationally. And it works for non-eBay transactions too.

# *18*

## *Global Payments*

Payments made globally have two major considerations, safety and currency exchange. eBay makes the exchange values simple by enabling buyers to see bids (prices) in their local currencies regardless of what a seller posts. Thus, an eBay seller doesn't have to post values in various currencies. PayPal, owned by eBay, makes transaction abroad safer, at least in the PayPal countries listed below. The payment risks are being reduced progressively by PayPal as it adds new countries and more features. And PalPay also provides convenience by doing currency exchanges as part of the PayPal transaction service.

145

# International Payments

You can receive payment for goods a number of different ways internationally. Each has its benefits and disadvantages.

## *Receiving Payment*

Currency exchange—a task of global commerce—is simple, right? You just accept payment in US Dollars, and buyers can make a currency exchange easily to pay you in US Dollars, right? Not exactly.

When someone pays you in one currency and you receive payment in another currency, or vice versa, the currency of the payer needs to be exchanged into the currency of the payee. Banks buy and sell currencies at wholesale exchange rates in increments of $1,000,000. At the consumer and small business level, the exchange rates are retail rates. In other words, currency exchanging costs money. The expense can be significant, especially if the seller must absorb it.

### *A Few Percent*

A small business can get nickeled and dimed to death (unprofitability) by small fees. A few percent here and a few percent there all adds up. The exchange rate is another one of those expenses that's "just" a few percent.

The question is, Who pays for the exchange? We contend that the buyer pays for the exchange if nothing is stated or agreed to the contrary. Indeed, this is the simplest way to make a transaction work.

## *The Price in US Dollars*

First, you need to state what is acceptable payment in your auction ad, particularly for potential buyers abroad. In other words, specifically state that payment is to be in US Dollars. Second, state the form of payment (e.g., money order). Here you need to broaden your horizon a little. You need to take into consideration what types of payments are feasible for buyers abroad. Third, you should probably warn buyers that to exchange into US Dollars will cost them something extra.

That puts the burden on buyers to pay according to your requested means of payment and to make arrangements to exchange their currency into dollars for whatever form of payment they use. Unfortunately, that inconveniences buyers, and you have to ask yourself whether that's good customer service.

## The Price in Foreign Currencies

Good customer service might be to accept the buyer's currency. How can you do this? Well, you can set up a bank account in the country into which you are selling goods via eBay. You can deposit payments made in that country's currency into that bank account.

Suppose you sell goods to international buyers via eBay US. You find that 35 percent of your sales are coming from Italy. It might be a good business plan to open a bank account in Florence and accept Euros thereby providing better customer service to your Italian customers.

If you set your prices in a foreign currency, however, where do you stop? Do you set it only in Euros and Pounds Sterling? Or, do you set it in Won, Yen, and Canadian Dollars too? And what about Rupees, Birrs, and Quetzals?

Then too, there's the question of how do you convert your price into a foreign currency. Do you do it the day you post your eBay auction ad at the current exchange rate, and post the price in the ad? Or, do you set the price to be calculated at the currency exchange rate the day that the auction is completed? It all gets so very complicated. (eBay actually displays prices in the home country currency of each eBay member. You need to investigate this more fully for each country to detemine whether it solves the problem.)

One way to do it would be to accept checks in any currency and run them through your bank. You would pay the currency exchange and perhaps additional bank charges. For high-profit items, it might be worthwhile.

# Actual Payment

What are the alternatives for payment? Below is a short list of the ways purchases abroad might be paid on eBay.

## Personal Check

Personal checks work. They take longer to clear internationally than they do locally, and the buyer might get tired waiting for the merchandise while the check clears. Your bank might have trouble reading a check in a foreign language. The seller pays for the currency exchange.

## Foreign Draft

If you need to write a check in a currency not your own, you ask your bank for a foreign draft. You pay for the currency exchange. A foreign draft is like a cashier's check. Don't count on every branch of a bank to do foreign drafts, and don't count on all banks (except the large ones) to do foreign drafts. Inquire ahead of the time you need it. The buyer pays for the currency exchange.

## Cashier's Check

A cashier's check in the seller's currency works. It's just like a personal check except it has more credibility. The seller pays for the exchange.

## Money Order

International postal, bank, and Western Union money orders are well used outside the US to pay for goods and services. Who pays for the currency exchange, the buyer or seller, depends on what currency a money order is in. This tends to be an expensive form of payment for low-price merchandise.

### Credit Card

Credit cards are handy because the currency exchange is built in as part of the process. The credit card companies do it for you. But they charge an exchange fee. The buyer pays for the exchange.

### PayPal

And, of course, don't overlook PayPal. It's a safe way to pay globally, at least in 38 countries. See Chapter 17 for PayPal Basics. See Chapter 19 for future PayPal possibilities. See the next section for PayPal basics for global eBay. The buyer pays for the currency exchange.

# PayPal International

PayPal now has members in 38 countries. The countries are listed below:

Anguilla*

Argentina*

Australia

Austria

Belgium

Brazil

Canada

Chile

China

Costa Rica*

Denmark

Dominican Republic*

Finland

France

Germany

Greece

Hong Kong

Iceland

India

Ireland

Israel

Italy

Jamaica*

Japan

Luxembourg

Mexico

Netherlands

New Zealand

Norway

Portugal

Singapore

South Korea

Spain

Sweden

Switzerland

Taiwan

United Kingdom

United States

(* cannot receive payments)

eBay bought PayPal in the fall of 2002 and expanded it abroad. eBay considers it a necessary cornerstone of eBay's expansion abroad.

## *Currency Exchanges*

PayPal enables payments in five currencies: US Dollars (USD), Canadian Dollars (CAD), Yen (JPY), Pounds Sterling(GPB), and Euros EUR). The countries that use Euros are: Austria, Belgium, Finland, France, Germany, Greece, Ireland, Italy, Luxembourg, Netherlands, Portugal, and Spain. But Denmark, Sweden, and the UK don't use Euros yet. They may decide to do so in the future. As more countries join the European Common Market (European Union), most will convert to Euros in the future in all likelihood. The new members to join in May 2004 were Cyprus, Czech Republic, Estonia, Hungary, Latvia, Lithuania, Malta, Poland, Slovakia, and Slovenia.

PayPal exchanges currency for you at retail exchange rates. Just like retail prices for goods vary, retail currency exchange rates vary too. PayPal claims to have low retail rates compared to other financial services. See Table 18.1 for the exchange rates for $1 US.

**Table 18.1 PayPal exchange rates for $1 US compared, on January 15, 2003.**

| Service | Canadian Dollars | Euros | Pounds Sterling |
|---|---|---|---|
| Western Union | 1.4737 | 0.8989 | 0.5866 |
| PayPal | 1.5007 | 0.9256 | 0.6104 |

As you can see, there's over a 2 percent difference between Western Union and PayPal on the chart. PayPal claims to add a 2.5 percent spread to the wholesale exchange rate it receives from its bank. But don't take PayPal's word for it—the figures are old. Shop around to see what it will cost you to exchange currency today. Try PayPal, your bank, your credit cards providers, Western Union, and other financial services. You can check the PayPal exchange rate anytime by using the PayPal currency converter on the PayPal website. PayPal plans to accept more currencies in the future with Australian Dollars being at the top of the list.

This is a great service for PayPal to offer. It makes purchases very convenient for buyers with different currencies than sellers. The fact that the exchange is made at a low retail currency exchange rate is an attractive feature of the service too.

You can also check exchange rates at eBay's convenient Universal Currency Converter (*http://pages.ebay.com/services/buyandsell/currency-converter.html*). Other websites have currency converters as well.

## PayPal As Usual

PayPal on the international scene is PayPal as usual. You can make payments and receive payments with greater safety. (Note that members in five countries cannot receive payments yet.) Nonetheless, many countries abroad are still far away in distance, culture, and law enforcement. Take all the normal precautions and use common sense.

# Summary

Global payments are becoming easier and more convenient at the same time they are becoming safer. There is still a long way to go to include all countries worldwide, but there is enough infrastructure in place already to expand your consumer sales with confidence. PayPal is the cornerstone of the new infrastructure.

# *19*

## *PayPal Import-Export*

This chapter is speculation. We're going to discuss some services that should exist but don't yet exist and some services that do exist and may be a substitute for traditional import-export services. But before this chapter will make any sense, you need to read Chapter 13 on letters of credit. It is letters of credit for which we seek a substitute. That is, it is contingent payment traditionally enabled by letters of credit for which we need a more modern process. Why? Letters of credit can be cumbersome and costly. Will there be a more efficient and less costly process for contingent payment in the future of importing and exporting? If there is, it could be a PayPal process.

This is all about making transactions secure for parties when they are borders apart in different countries. You have read in Chapters 17 and 18 how PayPal makes transactions secure within the US and in many additional countries. Most of those techniques are designed for consumer transactions. Many work well globally as well as in the US. But what we are speculating about in this chapter are business transactions and large transactions where the parties desire stricter security and less risk.

# Contingency Payments

What's a contingency payment? It's a payment that is not made until a condition is met by the beneficiary (payment recipient – seller).

## *Small Businesses*

Small firms in the import-export business have traditionally used letters of credit to make contingent payments. The buyer (small business) buys a letter of credit from a bank. The letter of credit is essentially a bank's promise to pay the seller (manufacturer or wholesaler in another country) if and when a condition is met. Typically the condition is the delivery of goods at a certain time and place. And typically the seller's bank collects the documentation which meets the condition (proves the condition is met), submits the documents to the buyer's bank, and receives the payment from the buyer's bank.

The contingent payment takes the risk out of the deal for both parties. The seller knows he will be paid when he delivers the goods because the letter of credit is a promise from a bank. The buyer knows she will get the goods because the seller won't get paid unless the seller delivers the goods. The banks have been using this system for a very long time, and there are experienced banks all over the world that make this system work.

What's wrong with this system? Well, most letters of credit are custom-made, which means each takes time and costs a lot. Letters of credit are normally handled by banks. (Not all banks handle letters of credit. Your bank may not. Thus, you may need to find a bank that does.) Where there's not much at stake, letters of credit still take time and cost money. Where's there's a lot at stake, even attorneys may get involved. That means more time and more money.

That's OK for big business and big deals. But we're interested in eBay businesses, which are primarily small businesses and small deals. Is it possible that a standard contingent payment process can be devised to accommodate global trade for small transactions, a contingent payment that is easy-to-arrange, quick, and inexpensive?

## Escrow and PayPal

One way to accomplish a contingent payment is a combination of PayPal and an online escrow company. The PayPal component is the means of payment. The escrow component handles the contingency. The buyer makes a payment to the escrow company via PayPal. The escrow company receives the money. When the condition is met by the seller to the satisfaction of the escrow agreement, the escrow company pays the seller.

What are the benefits and disadvantages?

### Benefits

PayPal saves the trouble, delay, and expense of a wire transfer. (If you don't start in the morning to arrange a wire transfer with a bank, you probably won't get it done that day. Afternoon may be too late.) An escrow company can normally handle a transaction quite efficiently.

### Disadvantages

This is not an ideal system for the following reasons:

- Escrow fees tend to be high, and they may not enable a reasonable cost savings.

- The payment mode (PayPal) and the contingency arrangement (escrow) are handled by separate online companies requiring coordination.

- An escrow company would have to develop experience in import-export to provide a reliable service.

- Online escrow companies still seem to be evolving and may not be ready for prime time yet on the global scene.

- It may be difficult to find an online escrow company willing to do business in a large number of different countries.

- Businesses in other countries may not trust online escrow companies in the US, or vice versa.

- So many eBay scams have involved phony online escrow companies lately that legitimate online escrow companies are being tainted by the fraud of others.

All things considered, it is premature to ascertain whether escrow companies can handle the import-export business.

## PayPal and Contingency Payments

What about PayPal itself? Could it develop a standard contingency procedure that would allow it to make delayed contingent payments? We think it could. Here's what it might look like:

- A standard, fill-in-the-blanks contingency agreement requiring the use of standard import-export documents, all published by PayPal as forms.

- Rules of procedure and standards for performance set by PayPal.

- Parties (buyers and sellers) more thoroughly authenticated by PayPal than they are currently.

- A reasonable processing fee.

- Upper limit on the transaction amount to accommodate small businesses but not large transactions.

PayPal is an ideal contingency payment service provider for the following reasons:

- It already operates in multiple countries (38) and with multiple currencies (5). More are being added.

- It is trusted.

- It is owned by eBay.

- It can develop an expertise in the import-export business quickly.

- It is widely popular in eBay commerce already.

So, it's up to PayPal (and eBay) to devise a way to put online contingent payments into the common commerce of small businesses desiring to start or expand into import-export activities.

## For Whom?

As we mentioned, a PayPal contingent payment system would be good for small businesses. What does that mean to PayPal members? Review our example in Chapter 13, buying 1,000 Madras shirts in India. That is a very realistic illustration of what a small business might import into the US to sell on eBay US. You might find yourself in a similar situation before long seeking a means of paying securely for a sizable amount of merchandise you intend to import and sell on eBay.

Remember, too, that small traditional import-export businesses will potentially find a PayPal contingency arrangement quite useful. After all, PayPal is not limited to eBay members nor limited to eBay transactions.

### Letter of Credit?

If PayPal were to develop a global contingency payment process for small businesses, perhaps it would be—after all—a letter of credit. If so, it might be a letter of credit along the lines of the online letter of credit offered by Secure LC at *http://www.securelc.com*. This is the online escrow-letter-of-credit service mentioned in Chapter 13. It provides online forms and charges a reasonable fee.

# New Currency

If you look at currency just as a means of exchanging value—a means of payment—then it's not such a jump in concept to see a payment process as a type of currency. This is particularly true when that process is very simple and easy to use. That raises the question, Will Pay-Pal become the new international currency for consumer transactions? If so, this possibility has tremendous potential to cause a revoluntion in international trade, particularly for consumer transactions. This possibility is particularly relevant to eBay and eBay members. Indeed, eBay, its members, and PayPal are breaking new ground here when using PayPal internationally. In other words, you're making history in this age of global commerce we are in now, and we believe it will pay off in a big way now and in the years ahead.

# Summary

The world waits for a new scheme of international contingent payments arranged and processed online for small businesses inexpensively. PayPal is the leading candidate to create and operate such a system.

In effect, PayPal is becoming the new international currency for global transactions. This will facilitate an expansion of international consumer transactions, an expansion which can benefit eBay members. Think of the possibilities!

# V

## Shipping

# 20

## Package Shipping

The package shippers internationally are known as *couriers*. They include:

DHL

Federal Express (FedEx)

Purolator

United Parcel Service (UPS)

The post office in every country also ships packages. In this chapter we cover:

Canada Post

US Postal Service

These governmental organizations have handled imports and exports for hundreds of years.

What do these all these organizations have in common? First, generally they all ship by air abroad. Second, their service is limited to packages that individual delivery people can carry. Consequently, you don't have to wait for surface shipping via the ocean. But you can't ship packages over about 150 pounds (or lower for some shipping services), and the packages are limited to certain dimensions.

Most eBay sellers will ship most individual items by either courier or post office. Consequently, this chapter is appropriate for most eBay commerce. Chapter 21 covers bulk shipments.

# Courier

A courier is a corporation that provides shipping for packages that individuals can handle. Or, at least that's the theory. We're not sure how many people can muscle around 150-pound packages, but most people can do so reasonably easily with the help of a hand truck.

### *Bigger and Heavier*

Actually, bigger and heavier packages may be more accepted for international transport than for domestic transport because there is no reasonably fast shipping alternative. Check all the couriers to determine what their latest guidelines are for package sizes and weights.

The couriers will pick up a package, fly it to the destination country, clear it through customs, and deliver it by truck to the buyer (consignee). These services are quick, reliable, and serve most of the world. Unfortunately, courier service tends to be relatively expensive and are not practical for most inexpensive items. For inexpensive items, the cost of shipping via courier can exceed the value of the item.

The major couriers are newcomers to global shipping by air (the first, FedEx started in the early 80s) and should not be confused with traditional courier services that were, and still are, more narrow in scope. Many small, specialized courier services still exist but are beyond the scope of this book. Many of the small courier services, because they do provide special services, are more expensive than the major couriers.

The major couriers generally provide more than just package shipping for sizable clients (e.g., medium and large corporations). They provide logistics systems and other services that most small eBay businesses cannot afford. But it's nice to know that such services are available should your volume grow large enough to justify the cost.

The major couriers are starting to look the same. DHL is a general shipping company that now offers courier services. FedEx and UPS are courier companies that now arrange general shipping too.

## *DHL*

This shipper in 2003 purchased the Airborne Express domestic surface delivery capability in the US, and now DHL has a strong toehold in the US market. DHL has always been strong internationally. Today it competes with FedEx and UPS who together have about 80 percent of the courier business. Consequently, DHL's slice of the market is from the remaining 20 percent.

Visit the DHL website (*http://www.dhl.com* or *http://www.dhl-usa.com*) for full information. DHL combines truck, rail, and ocean freight with its air freight service to provide you with full-service shipping if you need it. In that way it differs from the other courier services (go to *http://www.dhl.com/PageLayout.svr?Option=3&Value=2.6Sort AZ&COUNTRY=g0&LANG=en* for a comprehensive list of services). But DHL provides courier service, too, and thus belongs in this chapter.

Interestingly, DHL now offers what it calls Trade Automation Service (TAS). This is a free service that purports to ensure that all packages have the documentation necessary for proper customs clearance in the destination country. DHL claims service to 220 countries.

DHL also offers a DHL toolbar for installation in your browser for easy access to DHL online services; and it provides a rate calculator at *http://www.dhl-usa.com/ratecalculator/HandlerServlet?client=RATE_DISPLAY.*

# FedEx

You can reach the international section of the FedEx website at *http://fedex.com/us/international/?link=1*. FedEx provides you with the Global Trade Manager.

## Four Steps

FedEx provides you with a four-step process for shipping your items at *https://gtm.fedex.com/us/international/shipguide/?link=4*.

### First Step

The first step provides you with:

- Country profiles
- Denied party screening
- Transit time
- Estimated duties and taxes

Each country profile has:

- Country information

- Trade group member

- General import clearance information

- General import prohibitions

- General import restrictions

- Special import provisions

- Standards

- General export clearance information

- General export prohibitions

- General export restrictions

- Regulatory contact information

You can also determine if any parties with whom you are dealing are on a country's black list (unacceptable trading partners).

FedEx also provides a calculator to determine transit time from one place to another. For example, a two-pound FedEx Express Pak from Kiev in the Ukraine to Caracas, Venezuela via FedEx International Priority takes seven days.

Finally, *FedEx will also estimate the duties and taxes you will have to pay on an import.* For instance, a coffee maker worth $350 US made in France and shipped from France to the US has a duty of $12.95 US to be paid to US Customs. This is a slick calculator that can save you a lot of time and effort.

### Second Step

The second step is the FedEx Ship Manager software. This enables you ship a package quickly. There's an online tutorial to help you learn how to use it. And it includes a rate calculator.

### Third Step

FedEx provides sample import documents for about 40 countries (more being added). A hard drive made in the US worth $80 and shipped to India for import there is required by customs in India to have a *commercial invoice*. But the US requires a *Destination Control Statement* for export. The Global Trade Manager gives useful supporting information for the documents required. This, too, is a slick online service that can save you time and effort.

### Fourth Step

Drop off the package with the proper documentation or have FedEx pick it up.

### Comments

This is a fabulous service. You can get all your bureaucratic work done here. It doesn't get much better than this.

## Other Services

You can track your shipment and get proof of delivery.

Run the demo on the first page of the Global Trade Manager and get a quick visual tour with a narrative of FedEx international services. It will get you off to a good start.

You can also visit the International Resource Center, which features:

- News center
- Tools
- Export/import instructions
- Customs resources
- Library of customs forms

FedEx has done a great job of providing a valuable overall service to those who desire to export.

## *Purolator*

Purolator is Canada's largest courier company and has a presence in the US too. For information visit the website at *http://www.purolator.com*. The information there is a little thin, but it does have a rate calculator. Purolator claims service to 220 countries and offers free customs brokerage service for certain express shipments, but not all shipments. Note that Canada Post owns about 94 percent of Purolator.

## *UPS*

UPS offers a website section devoted to International Trade at *http://www.ups.com/content/us/en/bussol/supply/international.html*. You can find the following there:

**Customs Brokerage** UPS has hundreds of licensed customs brokers in its offices around the country to take care of your customs clearance.

**Compliance Consulting** UPS will help you develop plans to implement a customs compliance program to streamline your clearance efforts.

**Trade Consulting** UPS can provide substantial information on customs requirements for every country.

**Tariff Consulting** UPS will help you determine and pay duties and otherwise assist you in complying with customs regulations.

**UPS Trade Direct** UPS will provide freight forwarding services to you.

You can also calculate the shipping rate for international shipments in the normal UPS rate calculator. UPS provides a broad range of international shipping services. If you use UPS domestically, you will find the shift to international shipping almost seamless.

For the finale, UPS now has a service to compete with the FedEx information service outlined above. This, too, is a useful service, which can make your job easier. It's the Global Advisor at *http://ups.com/globaladvisor*. It includes a time and cost calculator, customs brokerage services, a list of prohibited items, export documentation and samples, and the like. Take advantage of the Global Advisor. It will save you a lot of time and effort.

# Post Office

The post office exists in every country. Countries have post office treaties with other countries. This scheme of treaties forms an international shipping system that is only as good as the post office organizations in each country. Quality varies. This system is not as reliable as the couriers, nor as fast. But it's less expensive, and it gets the job done most of the time.

Note that both Canada Post and USPS are participants in the annual eBay Conference.

## *USPS*

A good place to start evaluating the robust international shipping services of the US Postal Service is at Global Delivery Services (*http://usps.com/global*). This will give you a taste of what you can expect to find (service, starting price, delivery time):

**Global Priority Mail**, $4 US, 4-6 days

**Global Economy** (Parcel Post), $15.25 US, 4-6 weeks

**Global Airmail** (Parcel Post), $12.50 US, 4-10 days

**Global Express**, $15.50 US, 3-5 days

**Global Express Guaranteed**, $36 US, 2-3 days

All except Global Priority Mail include a return receipt. In addition, the Postal Service offers business mailing services for document mailing.

You can go to the International Rate Tables (*http://usps.com/global/intlratetables.htm*) to estimate the cost of shipping. The International Resource Center (*http://usps.com/global/intlresourcecenter.htm*) provides a wealth of services similar to those offered by the couriers such as calculators, forms, and customs clearance. Fees for customs clearance range from $5 CA in Canada to $21+ US in Switzerland and are passed on to the destination countries. Although the post office is reputed to be the least expensive shipping alternative, it isn't always. You will want to compare rates with the couriers.

The International Mail Manual is online at *http://pe.usps.gov/text/imm/welcome.htm*. It will help you with the details should you do much shipping via the Postal Service.

USPS also selects and qualifies wholesalers, companies that offer mail services. You can work with these companies to get expanded services beyond what USPS offers yet still use USPS.

### Free Pickup

USPS has a free daily pickup service (at the same time your mail is delivered). You have to notify USPS one day ahead. USPS also has a Pickup on Demand service for which it charges a fee.

## Canada Post

Canada Post (*http://canadapost.com*) is the Canadian post office and has international services that can benefit even US eBay sellers. After all, Canada is currently the largest eBay market outside the US for US sellers. Canada Post will clear customs for a $5 CA fees for items with values under $1,600 CA.

For Canadian eBay sellers, Canada Post provides services comparable to USPS and even provides courier service via Purolator in which it owns a controlling interest.

For information on sending parcels internationally go to *http://canada-post.com/business/prodserv/sp/int/default-e.asp*. The website even has a list of international post offices where postal service is *not* available. For international rates go to *http://canadapost.com/business/rates/int/default-e.asp*. There are informative sections on Sending to Canada and on Sending to the US.

# eBay Auction Ads

For your eBay auction ad, you need to make a decision. Are you going to ship to high bidders (buyers) abroad. If not, state so in your ad. If so, state that you will ship worldwide. If you're not willing to ship worldwide, state where you will ship. This will save you considerable email correspondence.

# Packaging

The couriers and post offices do a good job today of handling packages without destroying them. Then too, professional packaging materials are readily available to everyone. When you send packages abroad via the couriers, you will have about the same experience with package damage as you do with the couriers at home. The post offices, however, transport their packages by more diverse means. You will want to make sure your packaging is adequate for the extra stress they will endure during longer transportation periods and over greater transportation distances.

### Rates

You will need the weight and the package dimensions (three dimensions) to determine a shipping rate for a particular package.

## *Adequacy*

Look for packaging guidelines on the courier and post office websites. The couriers and post offices also provide packaging materials, free for many shipping services. *eBay the Smart Way* Third Edition provides information on shipping and packaging too. And, of course, eBay is a great place to buy shipping and packaging materials inexpensively.

---

**Stores**

---

UPS now owns Mailboxes, Etc and the name has been changed to UPS Store. FedEx owns Kinkos. Packaging service is available at both of these store chains.

---

DHL provides robust packaging advice on its website. You can start with the following page

**Packaging Advice,** *http://www.dhl.com/PageLayout.svr?COUN-TRY=g0&LANG=en&ID=5.2ShpInfIdx&Option=4&Value=3*

which will lead you to the following pages:

**General Packaging Tips,** *http://www.dhl.com/PageLay-out.svr?COUNTRY=g0&LANG=en&ID=5.2.3PkgAdvIdx& Option=4&Value=1*

**Internal Packaging,** *http://www.dhl.com/PageLayout.svr?COUNT RY=g0&LANG=en&ID=5.2.3PkgAdvIdx&Option=4&Value=3*

**External Packaging,** *http://www.dhl.com/PageLayout.svr?COUNT RY=g0&LANG=en&ID=5.2.3PkgAdvIdx&Option=4&Value=2*

**Packaging Specific Products,** *http://www.dhl.com/PageLay-out.svr?COUNTRY=g0&LANG=en&ID=5.2.3PkgAdvIdx& Option=4&Value=4*

These complex links may change, but you will find this information somewhere on the DHL website, and it's worthwhile finding it.

FedEx also provides packaging guidelines at *http://fedex.com/us/services/ground/packaging*, and eBay provides a packing guide in its Shipping Center (*http://pages.ebay.com/services/buyandsell/shipping.html*).

Packaging for bulk shipping (see Chapter 21) is usually no different than packaging for items that one person can handle. The packaged goods are placed in a metal cargo container. For large or heavy items, you may need special packaging such as custom-built crates and the like.

## *Documentation*

Remember from Chapter 6 that the proper documents must go in an envelope attached to the outside of the package. Otherwise the package cannot clear customs. This is true regardless of how the package is shipped.

## Summary

Your best bet for shipping is to compare rates, services, and reliability. This is a competitive business. Don't assume that the post office will always beat the couriers in price and scope of global operations. Don't assume that the couriers will always beat the post office in services. Take the time to do some ongoing comparative shopping.

# *21*

## *Bulk Shipping*

Shipping in bulk is generally for shipping items that the courier services or post office won't ship. In other words, if one delivery person can't move it, it has to be delivered by a trucking company, not a courier delivery truck. Most likely it will go abroad via surface shipping (i.e., via ship), but it could be shipped by air too. Bulk shipping also includes shipping multiple items at the same time. Most bulk shipping is in cargo containers.

For instance, suppose you ship a Toro tractor (used to cut grass on large lawns) from the US to Costa Rica. It weighs 320 pounds. You can't ship it via normal courier service. It's too heavy to ship by air economically. You will probably ship it by ship in a crate inside a cargo container. Suppose you ship 1,000 stereo amplifiers from Singapore to the US. They weigh 4 pounds each (total 2 tons). Shipping them individually by courier would be too expensive and an administrative nightmare. You will probably ship them by ship in multiple boxes inside cartons, all inside a cargo container.

Bulk shipping is generally the most economical means of shipping large, heavy, or multiple-item shipments. It goes primarily by surface (truck, rail, and ship), but sometimes by air. It is generally more risky and slower than shipping by courier.

Bulk shipping is more risky because it's in the shipping system longer, usually travels via more carriers, is passed through more shipping companies, and is handled more often. In contrast, a courier package is handled by only one company from beginning to end in a quick shipment. Although shipping by surface is slower than by air for obvious reasons, it is much faster today than in times past. In 1967 Joe shipped a 75-pound wooden elephant from Bangkok to Detroit. It took eight months. Today such a shipment would not be likely to take more than eight weeks.

# Containers

A good place to for specific information on ocean-going containers is the *Dictionary of International Trade* Fifth Edition, Hinkelman, World Trade Press, Novato California, 2002. It shows detailed specifications for the following (length in feet).

- General container 20/40
- High cube general container 40
- Hardtop container 20/40

- Open top container 20/40

- Flat bed container 20/40

- Platform container 20/40

- Insulated container 20/40

- Ventilated container 40

- Bulk container 20

- Refrigerated container 20/40

- High cube refrigerated container 40

- Tank container 20

Most of these containers have a width and height of about 7.5 feet. The high cube and open top containers have a height of almost 9 feet. The maximum weight capacity of a 20-foot container is about 21 tons and a 40-foot container about 33 tons.

The *Dictionary* also shows detailed specifications for unit load devices (ULD) used for air freight. Some are netted metal pallets from 60 to 96 inches wide, 125 to 238 inches long, and 64 to 188 inches high. Others are actual metal boxes in various shapes to fit the interior of specific jet aircraft. They range from 60 to 96 inches wide, 61 to 186 inches long, and 64 to 96 inches high. They have a maximum weight capacity from 2.25 to 15 tons.

This will give you an idea of how bulk cargo is shipped, even though you are unlikely to make a bulk shipment that fills one cargo container.

Let's review the examples above, the Toro tractor and the 1,000 stereo amplifiers. Neither of these shipments will come close to filling an ocean-going cargo container. The 1,000 stereo amplifiers will come close to filling the smallest ULD, but there will still be room to spare.

Do you have to pay for the full cargo container when you only use a portion of it?

That's where freight consolidators enter the picture. They arrange for your shipment to be put in a cargo container with other shipments for other companies. This makes your shipping cost much more economical. Remember from Chapter 8 that customs brokers and freight forwarders today will do freight consolidation for you. They will get you a lower shipping rate based on sharing a cargo container with other shipments.

Cargo container transportation is an efficient global shipping system today. It generally moves cargo much faster than in the days before the widespread use of cargo containers. Consequently, you can rely upon getting your shipment to its destination in a reasonably short time and even a reasonably predictable time.

# Incoterms 2000

These are international standard terms of trade commonly used in offers to sell or in sales contracts. They are published by the International Chamber of Commerce (*http://www.iccwbo.org/incoterms/ understanding.asp*). The latest edition of these terms was published in 2000. The use of these terms is both technical and legalistic. They are quite complex. They are included here not to help you use them but simply to help you recognize them when you run across them.

For a more thorough discussion of these terms try the *Dictionary of International Trade* mentioned above or go directly to the Incoterms 2000 website at the URL above.

Why are the Incoterms 2000 included in this chapter of the book? Well, when you read the terms, they tell you what responsibility you have to get the goods to the destination where you will store them or sell them. This can mean a little bit of extra expense or a substantial amount of extra expense depending on the terms.

For instance, EXW tells you that the manufacturer (wholesaler) makes the goods available at its factory (warehouse) at the price quoted. It's up to you—and it's your expense—to ship the goods to wherever they need to go, clear them through customs for import, and pay shipping insurance. In other words, the manufacturer (wholesaler) offers to deliver the goods to you at its factory (warehouse). The rest is up to you.

Below we use the term *seller* to denote a manufacturer, wholesaler, or exporter that owns the goods. The *buyer* is the person or company that will import the goods into the US.

These terms indicate a division of shipping cost, risk (insurance), and responsibility for clearing customs between the seller and the buyer. They are much more complex than defined here. But the following simplified definitions will give you an idea of the obligations that these terms set.

Keep in mind that a typical shipment has three legs. The first is transportation to the ship or airplane that will carry the goods abroad. The second is the transportation abroad by sea, air, or rail. The third is the transportation from the ship, airplane, or freight train to the final destination.

The Incoterms 2000 are divided into terms for any mode of transportation and terms limited to sea and inland waterway transportation.

## Any Transportation

The transportation covered below can include air, rail, truck, sea, or a combination thereof.

### EXW

The seller delivers the goods to buyer at the seller's place of business (EX Works *[named location]*). The buyer is responsible for all shipping and insurance. Example: *EXW Ex Works Plastico Factory Rosario Argentina*

## FCA

The seller delivers the goods to buyer's choice of shippers after clearing the goods for export (Free Carrier *[place]*). The buyer is responsible for shipping and insurance thereafter. Example: *FCA Free Carrier Smithwick Freight Forwarders Bucharest Romania*

## CPT

The seller delivers the goods to the shipper after clearing the goods for export (Carriage Paid To *[destination]*). The seller is responsible for shipping the goods to the named destination, but the buyer pays for the insurance for the sea or air transportation and for the remaining shipping to the final destination. This is used for air and other transport, not necessarily ocean transport. Example: *CPT Carriage Paid To Denver Colorado USA*

## CIP

The seller delivers the goods to the shipper after clearing the goods for export (Carriage and Insurance Paid To *[destination]*). The seller is responsible for shipping and insurance to the named destination. The buyer is responsible for the remaining shipping to the final destination. This is used for air and other transport, not necessarily ocean transport. Example: *CIP Carriage Paid To Tulsa Oklahoma USA*

## DAF

The seller delivers the goods to a named place after clearing the goods for export (Delivered At Frontier *[place]*). The named place can be in either the country of origin or the US. The buyer is responsible for shipping and insurance beyond the named place. *Example: DAF Delivered At Frontier New York New York USA*

### DDU

The seller delivers the goods at a named destination after clearing the goods for export (Delivered Duty Unpaid *[destination]*). Example: *DDU Delivered Duty Unpaid Columbus Ohio USA*

### DDP

The seller delivers the goods to a named destination after clearing the goods for both export and import (Delivered Duty Paid *[destination]*). Example: *DDP Delivered Duty Paid Charlotte North Carolina USA*

## Sea Transportation

The transportation covered below includes only water transportation, both sea and inland waterway.

### FAS

The seller delivers the goods alongside the ship on which they will be transported after clearing the goods for export (Free Alongside Ship *[port]*). The buyer is responsible for shipping and insurance thereafter and getting the goods on board the ship. Example: *FAS Free Alongside Ship Singapore*

### FOB

The seller delivers the goods aboard the ship on which they will be transported after clearing the goods for export (Free On Board *[port]*). The buyer is responsible for shipping and insurance thereafter. Example: *FOB Free On Board Saldanha South Africa*

### CFR

The seller delivers the goods aboard the ship on which they will be transported and to the destination port after clearing the goods for export (Cost and Freight *[port of destination]*). The buyer pays the insurance for the ocean shipping and is responsible for offloading the goods from the ship and for the remainder of the shipping and insurance once the ship reaches the destination port. Example: *CFR Cost and Freight Miami USA*

## CIF

The Seller delivers the goods aboard the ship on which they will be transported and to the destination port after clearing the goods for transport (Cost, Insurance and Freight *[port of destination]*). The buyer is responsible for offloading the goods from the ship and for the remainder of the shipping and insurance once the ship reaches the destination port. However, the buyer has an insurable interest for the ocean voyage. Example: *CIF Cost, Insurance and Freight Port of Long Beach*

## DES

The seller delivers the goods on board ship in the port of destination after clearing the goods for export (DES Delivered Ex Ship *[port]*). The buyer is responsible for offloading the goods from the ship and for shipping and insurance thereafter. Example: *DES Delivered Ex Ship Port of Boston*

## DEQ

The seller delivers the goods on the wharf in the port of destination after clearing the goods for export (DES Delivered Ex Quay *[port]*). The buyer is responsible for shipping and insurance thereafter. Example: *DES Delivered Ex Quay Houston Texas USA*

# Summary

When you can't ship by courier or via the post office, you have to ship in bulk. That invariably means a consolidated shipment in a cargo container on a ship, airplane, truck, or freight train. When you see an international offer on goods from a manufacturer or a wholesaler, the Incoterms 2000 used in the offer will give you specific information on who pays for shipping and insurance.

# 22

## *Insurance*

Never assume that you have insurance coverage for the shipment of goods. Always get a documentary record of the insurance coverage for each shipment and review it to make certain that coverage is adequate. If coverage isn't adequate, arrange additional insurance before the shipment. This all seems sensible and easy enough to do, but it is complicated by the fact that the services you will use (e.g., freight forwarding, customs brokerage, etc.) usually provide insurance—but not always.

In the US, sellers sometimes get careless about insurance. FedEx and UPS are secure. In addition, they provide minimal insurance. So, you only worry about insurance when you ship something extra valuable. Then you can purchase extended insurance just by requesting it on the shipping form. The US Postal Service is less secure and does not provide insurance. You can purchase it separately, but it's not cheap.

It seems to be the attitude of eBay sellers that it's the buyer's responsibility to get insurance. This is terrible customer service, and a seller will invariably get negative feedback if a buyer doesn't get delivery of an item and there is no insurance to cover it. Yet many buyers elect not to pay for insurance, potentially exposing sellers to bad PR.

Smart sellers will self-insure for inexpensive items. In other words, they will simply replace a missing shipment at their own expense. And they will include insurance as part of the shipping cost on valuable items.

Nonetheless, in the US these are not big issues because the shipping system is secure. You can afford to be careless about insurance, at least for inexpensive items.

# Abroad

When shipping abroad, however, the risk is higher as discussed in Chapter 21. Courier shipping is probably not much more risky abroad than in the US or Canada. But post office shipping is not as secure nor is bulk shipping. All require routine insurance coverage to carry on import-export activities safely.

## *Couriers*

Couriers provide minimal insurance coverage, usually $100. Their international shipping—indeed each of their different international shipping options—provides different basic coverage. You will have to study their coverage to understand just how much additional coverage you may need, if any. The minimal insurance of some couriers is not adequate for items that have much value, and you will have to get additional shipping insurance coverage. All the couriers offer additional insurance at additional cost.

## Post Office

The US Postal Service provides parcel insurance. Go to *http:// usps.com/global/intlspecialservices.htm* for rates. The upper limit is $1,000.

Canada Post gives coverage of $100 CA on international packet shipments. Go *http://www.canadapost.ca/business/offerings/small_packets/ int/features-e.asp* for additional information.

## Do It Yourself

Want to try a third-party insurance provider? It's always prudent to shop. Go to Universal Parcel Insurance Coverage at *http://www.u-pic.com*. They claim lower rates than the couriers offer. This is a competitive market. Keep yourself informed and up to date.

## Freight Forwarders

Remember in Chapter 8 we said that freight forwarders will take your shipments all the way from the origin to the destination using multiple modes of transportation. That includes taking care of the insurance too. Freight forwarders usually have a type of blanket insurance coverage to which they specifically add your shipment at the origin and subtract it at the destination. The result to you is often less expensive coverage.

Again, make sure you have documents from the freight forwarder stating that your shipment has insurance coverage. Don't take it for granted.

## *Customs Brokers*

Again, in Chapter 8 we said that today freight forwarders do customs clearance just like customs brokers and that many customs brokers do freight forwarding just like freight forwarders. In other words, these two services have merged in most firms. Consequently, you can expect customs brokers to take care of insurance coverage for you when preforming freight forwarding services. But don't take it for granted. Make sure you have coverage.

Not all customs brokers have changed with the times to provide freight forwarding services. Many small firms still do only customs brokerage. You cannot expect such firms to provide you with shipping insurance.

## *Managing General Agent*

A managing general agent is not an insurance company nor an insurance agent. It is somewhere in between. An example is Insure-Cargo.com (*http://insurecargo.com*), which will insure one shipment on what's called a stray risk policy. This is probably not an option for most eBay businesses except for large shipments. The minimum premimum is about $250 (for one shipment). InsureCargo partners with ACE (see below) for ocean cargo and Fireman's Fund for single shipments to provide insurance.

## *International Bulk Shipping*

International bulk shipping is primarily transportion by ship overseas. The best and least expensive way to insure it is through a marine insurance company like ACE USA, which owns Indemnity Insurance of North America (*http://ace-ina.com*). You pay for an open-ocean cargo policy, and the company tailors your insurance to your particular risk situation. This is financially feasible only for a substantial volume of ongoing shipping, however, as the minimum annual premium is about $10,000.

# Agreement

Who pays for the insurance depends on the agreement between the buyer and seller. They can have an agreement tailored to their individual needs, or they can use standard agreements as defined by the Incoterms 2000 (see Chapter 20). The risk of damage and loss can be divided many ways, and whoever has the risk for the entire transportation or a portion thereof needs to get insurance coverage.

# Summary

Shipping services are growing more robust and more specialized to meet expanding global business and consumer demands. They are also growing more complex. Woven somewhere into the rate structure and feature set of each package shipping service is the insurance feature—or the lack thereof. Analyze each service carefully so you can determine whether you have insurance coverage or not.

When making bulk shipments, you are undoubtedly best off in the hands of a freight forwarder or a customs broker doing freight forwarding that will provide you with insurance coverage. For an especially large one-time shipment for which you're managing the transportation, a managing general agent is a good place to get insurance. If you have ongoing bulk shipments, you can save money by getting an open ocean cargo policy.

---

Packaging

---

Make sure your packaging is adequate. See Chapter 20. If not, you may have a difficult time collecting on an insurance claim.

---

# VI

## Business and Culture

# *23*

# *Communication*

Communicating with the other party is crucial to a successful eBay transaction, even if it's just an impersonal form email. When problems arise, you can often solve them with an exchange of email. When a transaction starts to unravel, however, the telephone is the best means of getting things straightened out. Unfortunately, communicating abroad is more complex than communicating at home, particularly when there is a language difference. This chapter provides information that can help your communicative efforts.

# Email

Email is a medium that we have grown to take for granted. It's a medium to handle cautiously, however, when doing business.

## *Unique URL*

Every URL everywhere on the Internet is unique. Your email service is at a unique URL (e.g., YourISP.com). Your email address is unique at your own Internet service provider (ISP). For instance, JimJohnson is a unique address at YourISP.com. Therefore, the specific email address JimJohnson@YourISP.com is unique worldwide regardless of language.

Because everyone has a unique email address, regardless of language, you can always send an email to any person for whom you have an email address. Whether they will understand it is another question. But at least they will get it.

## *Convenience?*

Email has proven to be a very convenient and inexpensive means of communication worldwide. It has, together with the Web, opened up new markets and new business opportunities for everyone in every country who has an Internet account. And eBay is right in the middle of this worldwide revolution. But isn't it interesting that the ideal eBay transaction doesn't use email?

Indeed, both buyers and sellers hope that eBay will work by itself. Buyers hope there's enough information in the eBay auction ad upon which to make a purchase decision without bothering to ask the seller questions. Sellers hope they provide enough information in the eBay auction ad that they don't get any pesky emails from buyers.

Alas, it's not a perfect world, and email saves the day. It provides a great means for buyers and sellers to talk with each other across the globe essentially free. When problems arise with a prospective transaction or with a committed transaction, buyers and sellers can work it out. But they would rather not have to use it.

Most eBay email communications are automatic ones that take place at the end of an auction. Most eBay sales proceed without any custom communication by either party.

That is, until you start selling abroad. Even when English is the common language, you will use more emails to make sales abroad. There are simply more problems to solve in the routine course of business. When there are language differences, it will take even more emails to do routine business, and you will have to translate the email messages going and coming. The cost of routine business in money and resources will go up.

## Email Tips

Here are some tips for using email for communicating with those who speak English as a second language and with those who don't speak English. Indeed, they are good tips for all email communications:

1. Don't use slang or abbreviations.

2. Use simple vocabulary, short words and short sentences.

3. Keep the email itself short.

4. Keep the email all business. (Don't potentially confuse the other person with non-business matters.)

5. Have respect for the other person. Give them the benefit of the doubt. Reread the eBay Community Values on the eBay website.

Many experienced eBay global sellers will argue with us on #4. Part of the fun of doing business abroad is making new friends, and that's OK. But there's a greater risk of misunderstanding when attempting to do business and to make new friends at the same time. Take care of business first, at least until the transaction is proceeding smoothly, before you start making non-business conversation.

Email is a harsh means of communication when using it personally. You have to be very careful when carrying on an email conversation with anyone discussing non-business matters, even your own country-men. That's why the telephone is always better for solving problems.

Differences in culture and language increase the risk of misunder-standing. Ironically, most people will give the other person the benefit of the doubt more generously if the other person is in another country or speaks another language. That's a good thing. Keep it in mind when you communicate across the globe.

# Telephone

Telephone is a high content medium of communication which con-veys more than just words. It's much better than email for resolving problems between buyers and sellers. And now it's inexpensive enough to use for such negotiation and also for running your business across the US. Even calling abroad can be cost-effective.

## Calling Abroad

To call abroad is easy. First you dial the International Access Code (IAC). For the US it is 011. Next you dial the country's international dialing code. For example, it's 86 for China. (See Appendix V for country dialing codes.) Next you dial the telephone number within the country (including the area or city code, if any).

Suppose you want to call someone in Shanghai, China from the US. Shanghai's city code in China is 21. You would dial as follows:

011  86  21  [Shanghai phone number]

Dialing the number is the easy part. Paying for the phone call is another story. But costs are coming down.

# *Vonage*

Vonage (*http://www.vonage.com*) is a voice-over-IP telephone service. This means that your phone calls go over the Internet. Joe has used Vonage since the spring of 2002 and finds it to be a robust, dependable, and inexpensive telephone service. It provides low-cost telephone rates to most countries abroad. Joe's wife spent two weeks in Singapore in 2003. He talked with her every night from the San Francisco Bay Area for 6 cents a minute via Vonage. (The Vonage Singapore rate is now 4 cents a minute.) She sounded like she was a half-mile away. Great quality! Check the latest international rates at the Vonage website.

Sample International Rates (US cents per minute)

| | |
|---|---|
| Berlin | 3 |
| Buenos Aires | 4 |
| Cairo | 16 |
| Hong Kong | 2 |
| Istanbul | 12 |
| Johannesburg | 8 |
| London | 2 |
| Manila | 17 |
| Mexico City | 7 |
| Mombai | 12 |
| Moscow | 9 |
| Paris | 2 |
| Rome | 2 |
| Sao Paulo | 5 |
| Singapore | 4 |

| Sydney  | 3 |
|---------|---|
| Taipei  | 5 |
| Tel Aviv | 4 |
| Tokyo   | 3 |
| Toronto | 0 |

Check Vonage for the latest rates.

As this book went to press, only US residents were able to get Vonage accounts. However, any Vonage account can be used anywhere in the world where a broadband Internet connection is available. And Vonage-to-Vonage calls are free regardless of location.

That means that you (as a US resident) can get a second Vonage account and let your partner in another country use it. You can talk to each other free over thousands of miles for as long as you desire.

How does Vonage work? Here are the connection steps:

1.  Connect your cable or DSL modem to your cable or DSL outlet.

2.  Connect a router to your cable or DSL modem using a network cable.

3.  Connect Vonage's black box (Cisco ATA-186, free) to the router using a network cable.

4.  Connect an ordinary telephone to the black box using a standard two-pair telephone wire.

Couldn't be easier. Just use your ordinary telephone as you normally do. (Note you also connect your PC to the router. The router gives your PC the best protection against hacking. You can buy home routers for under $60.)

Vonage also has many frills that are potentially useful for business and global business. Take a good look at them on the Vonage website.

Vonage also has competitors. Voice-over-IP is a relatively new business that's starting to heat up. By the time you read this, many competitors to Vonage may have materialized (e.g., see Packet 8 below). Keep in mind that Vonage provides a full phone service. Lesser voice-over-IP services that cannot be considered full phone services already populate the Internet, and some have been around longer than Vonage.

Note that Vonage also offers 800 lines so that your customers can call you free. Great customer service!

## Voice-Over-IP

In addition to Vonage you might check on the following voice-over-IP services:

**Dialpad** (*http://dialpad.com*) You use your PC and a headset (earphones and microphone) to make calls to any phone anywhere using a dial-up Internet connection. The rates are low, particularly the international rates. There is a phone-to-phone service, too, with low rates. DialPad also offers a broadband service using a Cisco ATA-186, which is higher quality.

**Net2phone** (*http://www.net2phone.com*) This is one of the oldest voice-over-IP providers. It provides consumer services similar to DialPad featuring low domestic and international rates. In addition, it offers its service through cable companies that provide broadband Internet service. Check with your cable company to see if this system is available to you.

**Packet 8** (*http://www.packet8.net*) Very similar to Vonage, Packet8 provides broadband services that you use with a normal phone. Compare their international rates with Vonage.

**Skype** (*http://skype.com*) The free service offered by Skype is hard to beat on price. This is essentially PC software that enables you to call anyone anywhere who also uses the Skype software on her PC. It requires a headset, but it does not require broadband. It claims to have higher quality than a traditional phone. This can be a great cost-saving service if you have a partner abroad who has a PC.

**ISPs** Several major internet service providers (ISPs) also offer voice-over-IP services, most of which work similar to Skype. In the near future, many more ISPs will offer such services. Take a close look at your ISP's offerings. You may have Voice-over-IP available today, perhaps free.

It's beyond the scope of this book to provide details on all the voice-over-IP services or even provide details on all of the phone programs offered by the companies that are covered. Check out each of the services mentioned. You will be surprised how low some of the rates are.

Voice-over-IP really makes it much less expensive for you to conduct eBay business abroad.

## Headset

For many of these services, you must use a headset to use the service comfortably with your PC. A headset consists of earphones together with a microphone. The headset cord plugs into the sound card in your PC. Good quality headsets are readily available from $10 to $50. They are quite comfortable to use, even for long calls.

Starting in 2001, Joe had to start using a headset with his normal telephone to do interviews on radio shows that plugged his eBay books. A headset delivers better quality sound to the radio station via the telephone than does a handset. Today Joe uses a headset for 75 percent of his routine telephone calls. He can talk and keep on working at the same time or at least keep his hands free. Headsets are great! Try one.

Note that if your voice-over-IP service uses a Cisco ATA-186 and a broadband connection, you use a regular telephone, not a headset. However, you can always get a headset for your regular phone too.

## Fax

Is fax still alive? We suppose it is in spite of all the different types of digital documents, all of which can be attached to an email message. Fortunately, some of the voice-over-IP providers mentioned in this section provide fax services too.

## International Businesspeople

Businesspeople abroad take note. Some of these voice-over-IP services may not be available to you in your country yet. However, you may be able to establish an account in the US. Once you have an account with a voice-over-IP provider, you may be able to use it anywhere (e.g., Vonage). Do you have a friend or colleague in the US who can establish an account for you?

## Resort to the Phone

As mentioned in the email section above, email is a harsh medium of communication. It's too easy to be misunderstood or to misunderstand and take offense. The same goes for the other person. You always have to be careful with email. Many of the natural communication cues we depend on when communicating with other people are simply missing from email.

Real talking is much better. Conversation by voice contains much more communication information than conversation via writing. Voice contains a wealth of cues. That's why it's always best to resort to the telephone to work out serious problems that you otherwise can't seem to work out. Voice-over-IP provides you with a reasonably inexpensive means of calling people when the going gets rough.

## Thinking Voice

The Thinking Voice service (*http://thinkingvoice.com/ products_and_services.htm*) puts a link in your aucton ad. A potential customer clicks on the link and gets a mini form for filling in a telephone number. When the customer submits the form with a telephone number, Thinking Voice automatically calls you and the potential customer. Once on the phone you can answer questions and provide whatever assisstance necessary to the customer. This inexpensive service is available only in the US and Canada now but will expand eventually abroad. It's a great way to provide customer service.

# Language

It's scary to think about doing business in another language that you don't speak. What do you do? There's no easy answer. It's probably not practical to do business in another language, unless the potential gross profits are great enough to cover the additional expenses you will incur to do routine translations.

## Strategy

When you need to communicate with someone who doesn't speak English, you need to develop a strategy. You have to decide how to handle translations.

### Dictionaries

There are dozens and dozens of language dictionaries online. Normally they don't get you through a translation effort, unless you know the language. But you never know when one might come in handy.

Foreignword (*http://www.foreignword.com*), free

From Language to Language (*http://www.langtolang.com*), free

Language Automation (*http://www.lai.com/glmain.html*), free

### Digital Translation

Digital translations are now available via the Web. You submit the text in English, and the program (embedded in the webpage) translates the text from your language into the language of your choice. Try the following:

Babel Fish Translation (*http://babelfish.altavista.com*), free

Free Translation (*http://www.freetranslation.com*), free

Google (*http://www.google.com/language_tools?hl=en*), free

Systran (*http://www.systransoft.com*), free

WorldLingo (*http://www.worldlingo.com/products_services/ worldlingo_translator.html*), free

Likewise, you can take a text communication expressed in a foreign language and submit it to the program, which will translate it into English.

Free Translation also provides paid translator services for those who need more than a simple free digital service. Google enables you to search in foreign language words at foreign Google websites. World-Lingo enables you to *chat* in ten languages.

How well do these digital translators work? Well, they get better every year—supposedly. But you don't want to bet your business on them. They might be OK to struggle through a transaction with one person (see the case study below). But they're not very efficient for a healthy volume of routine business. And they might easily lead to a misunderstanding that would kill a transaction. Give them a try, but don't base your business plan on them until you become confident that they can do what you need them to do.

## Translator for Writing

What about a real translator? That's reasonably easy for writings. Just hire someone. They can do the translations wherever they office and send them to you via email. If you're on a budget, you might try hiring a college student. If you have a lot of volume, you might want to hire a full-time translator. Or, try a translation service, such as Free Translation mentioned above. One of the following translation services might be useful:

Applied Language Solutions (*http://www.appliedlanguage.com*)

HumanTran (*https://www.tranexp.com/win/HumanTran.htm*)

Online Language Translators (*http://www.online-languagetranslators.com*)

Proz (*http://proz.com*)

VeriTranslate (*http://www.veritranslate.com*)

## Translator for Conversation

A translator for conversation, now that's a different story. Unlike a translator for writing, a translator for speaking must be present for the communication (conversation). If you want to speak with someone abroad at 10:00 AM on Wednesday morning, the translator must translate at that time. He doesn't necessarily need to be present in your office. You can bring the translator into the conversation via a conference telephone call. After all, the person with whom you are communicating will be abroad somewhere. But the translator must be available at that particular time.

If you want to have a face-to-face conservation with someone at 10:00 AM on Wednesday morning, the translator must be present as well wherever the meeting is held.

A translator for conversation must be fluent as well as be available at the time needed. It's a higher level of skill to be fluent in speaking than in writing, except for foreign natives residing in the US. Consequently, a translator for conversation is likely to be more expensive than one for writing.

Again, some of the translation services mentioned above might be a good place to find a translator. Still, you might have better luck seeking a translator locally, particularly if you office in a large city.

Hang out on the eBay International Trading Discussion Board. You will find fellow eBay retailers ready to provide translation services for you on a volunteer basis. You can't build a business depending on volunteers, but one of those volunteers might be willing to provide ongoing translation services for pay.

## Employee

If you have the volume (or potential volume), you can justify hiring a translator to work full time. This approach satisfies all circumstances.

As pointed out in *eBay Business the Smart Way*, however, having an employee may not be the wisest way to have people do work for you. Contracting with an independent contractor to translate for you almost full time may be a better arrangement for you than hiring an employee.

# Consumer Case Study

(Told by Joe in the first person) While surfing on the Web one evening at a clothing vendor in England, I ran across an English oilcloth bush hat that intrigued me. Because I trek in the canyons in Utah and Arizona and climb mountains in Colorado, it looked like a suitable hat for my outdoor activities. But they didn't sell one big enough for me. (I take a 7 7/8 size, which translates to XXL. The English vendor offered only an XL.) So, I thought, why not look on eBay UK; and I did. Nothing there.

### One Reason

One reason I didn't take the risk that the available XL size might fit me, as it sometimes does, is that there is a 17 percent VAT in the UK. That added enough to the price (+$10) that it discouraged me, even though the vendor may not have charged the VAT to my purchase.

## *eBay France*

Then I thought, why not look on eBay France for a bush hat? I have often said that my high school French teacher Mr. Henry taught me more than any other teacher, but he didn't teach me much French. He was very urbane and sophisticated. Then in college I had to take an additional year of French for which I received my lowest college grade. But undaunted by my abject failure in French, I thought why not try to find a bush hat on eBay France. After all, I'm writing a book on global eBay. I'll just gut it out. Thus, duty called, and I went forth never anticipating how much fun it would be. It was great fun!

First, I placed the word *chapeau* (French for hat) in the search window. It was a major victory just to remember the word and spell it properly. Moreover, eBay France works exactly like eBay US, except that the words are in French. So, I felt right at home. About the tenth item (hat) from the top of the page, strangely enough, was a new French army hat very similar to a bush hat.

Although identical hats are readily available in the US and not something I would normally buy, I rushed into this new-found purchasing project with determination. I immediately checked what payment was acceptable. The seller didn't accept PayPal. So, I sent him an email. Hey, my eBay ID and password worked on eBay France!

First, of course, I went to Babel Fish, opened two browser windows to access an English-French translator in one window and a French-English translator in the other. The next step was to ask the seller in French if he would take PayPal. If not, would he take my personal check? I also mentioned that I didn't speak French and that I was using a software translator.

I was very proud of myself for having pulled off this amazing feat. Then I remembered that the auction was ending in 17 hours making matters even more complicated because I thought I may not get a reply within 17 hours. As a result, I had to send the seller another message (ah, those crazy Americans) saying that I noticed that the auction had only 17 more hours and that I would make a bid, even though I didn't know what payment he would accept.

The minimum bid was 10,00 Euros, about $12. (Notice that there's a comma after the ten, not a decimal point.) I bid 11,67 Euros. In two days I would know what the seller would do.

I had lots of fun. Even though my French was very rusty, I could tell that the English-French Babel Fish translations would be understood. And the French-English translations of the text in the seller's ad, although not perfect, were understandable too. It seemed to me that I could shop on eBay France all day and make some purchases. Indeed, there are a lot of French products I like very much. The next time I'm ready to buy one, I'll go back to eBay France.

### *Do Foreign Products Cost Too Much in the US?*

Some American importers don't bother to find wholesalers abroad. They just buy foreign products at retail and give them a standard markup to sell at home. The result is that the American importers sell in the US at a price about double the retail price abroad. Many Americans are willing to pay high prices for unique and elegant foreign products that have snob appeal. That's great for sellers.

Buyers, however, can now go right to the source. They can buy from foreign online storefronts, or they can buy on the eBays outside the US. To buy on the English-language eBays is easy. eBay works much the same everywhere. To buy on foreign-language eBays is more difficult but not impossible.

And now we return to the French army hat purchase story. How did my purchase turn out? Two days later I checked. Nothing happened. The auction ended; I was outbid; and the seller didn't bother to reply to my email.

But I was not to be denied. What could I do now but return to eBay France and try again? That's exactly what I did. This time—a little less excited—instead of trying to buy a hat that I really didn't want, I found a hat that I thought my daughter might like. Her birthday was coming up soon. I bid on it. I got a bid confirmation *in English*, and everything seemed to proceed smoothly.

### In English?

Yes, indeed. My bid confirmations for my bids on eBay France came to me in English as did all other automatically generated email from eBay France.

## Broken Ice

eBay France was the ice breaker. After my French connection, I looked for a bush hat on eBay Germany, eBay Italy, and eBay Mercado Libre (South America). Using Babel Fish for translation, it was great fun. I even bid and got outbid (in Spanish) in an auction on Mercado Libre.

Note that eBay Italy and many other eBays look exactly like eBay US. Mercado Libre, in which eBay has a minority investment, looks different. Mercado Libre is a little more difficult to use because it's not the same format as eBay.

### Enthusiasm

You can work up a lot of enthusiasm for personal shopping on eBays abroad. It's great fun. Don't let that lead you to the conclusion, however, that you can efficiently use a software translator like Babel Fish to make retail sales efficiently on eBays abroad with buyers who don't speak English. It will probably take more time than you're willing to spend, and the translations may cause more misunderstandings than you're willing to risk.

## *My Daughter's Hat*

Back to my daughter's hat on eBay France. I won the bidding. I communicated with the seller, who spoke no English, via email with translations via Babel Fish. He agreed to accept my personal check. I actually mailed him a bank cashier's check for the dollar equivalent calculated with an online currency converter. (In this case, the seller paid for the currency conversion.) He mailed the hat to me without waiting for the check to clear. I got the hat about two weeks later. The hat cost 10,00 Euros, and the mailing cost 5,00 Euros. It's a cute hat and typically French (see Figure 23.1).

**Figure 23.1    A French hat for my daughter.**

Note that I went to the local branch of my bank, a huge West Coast bank. I asked for a foreign draft in Euros. The teller didn't know what a Euro was, but the branch manager told me I could get the foreign draft by driving to downtown San Francisco to the main branch. That was an interesting bit of information indicating that banks are not yet set up in the branches for handling eBay consumer commerce abroad. Thus, I got a cashier's check in dollars and sent it in the mail to France.

## Summary

Going back to Chapter 1, you will note that over a billion people speak English. Hey, that's not a bad market! If you can't make a profit selling to a billion people, you probably can't make a profit selling to anyone. Do you really have to wrestle with all the problems of languages? Probably not. A reasonable strategy might be to ignore all opportunities abroad where language presents a problem (e.g., China where even the characters are different). There are plenty of opportunities where English is spoken and language is not a severe problem.

Nevertheless, such a simplistic strategy doesn't always work, and you may find yourself facing language as a barrier to your success. That's the time to develop a strategy for translations. In the meanwhile, email and voice-over-IP will do just fine for inexpensive English language communication worldwide.

# 24

## *Business Culture and Travel Abroad*

The stories of language and cultural disconnects abroad in business and marketing are legend. General Motors commenced its Chevrolet Nova car marketing campaign in Latin America not realizing that Nova means "no go" in Spanish. Pepsi commenced its cola marketing campaign in Taiwan with the slogan Pepsi Comes Alive. It was translated into Chinese with the literal meaning "Pepsi brings your ancestors back from the grave." These language faux pas are really marketing mistakes, not just language mistakes. They represent the failure of Chevrolet and Pepsi to take the time and effort to study the culture and develop unique local marketing campaigns in each world region where they sell their products. But you can learn the basic cultural byways, if not the language, before you visit a country. If you do, you will find the going much smoother in business.

### National Holidays

Check the national calendars of the countries you will visit. Go to Earth Calendar (*http://www.earthcalendar.net/index.php*) or Bank Holidays of the World (*http://www.national-holidays.com*) for comprehensive lists of national and religious holidays, which you can search several ways. You will want to coordinate your visits to avoid national holidays during which business and government offices will not be open.

# Why Travel?

Ah, today with the Internet and a world of information at your finger tips, why take an expensive trip abroad? You can develop foreign business and tend it from home, can't you? Not easily. Your best shot at

- Finding new products
- Finding manufacturers and wholesalers
- Finding joint venturers
- Discovering and evaluating new markets
- Better understanding existing markets abroad
- Shopping for saleable products
- Making useful contacts
- Acquiring useful information

is by traveling to another country. It should be a country where you are doing business, would like to do business, or would like to check out in regard to doing business.

## Better Than a Trade Show

Import-export shows and industry trade shows in the US that include manufacturers from abroad are good places to do all the things mentioned above. But it's never quite the same as going to another country, particularly if you can attend an industry trade show in the other country as part of your visit. There is something about being there that is more productive than staying home.

## Tax Write-Off

And besides, one of the benefits to you as an eBay entrepreneur is the capability to enjoy travel abroad and expense the trip on your income tax return (perfectly legal). If you're in the 28 percent tax bracket, you travel in effect at a 28 percent discount.

# Planning and Preparation

It's fun to travel whether for business or pleasure, but to make it productive and fun, you have to plan your trip.

## Language

If you do business in one country abroad regularly, you can take the time to learn the language more than just superficially. And it will pay dividends in your business relationships. When you do business in multiple countries, all with different languages, you will probably never learn the languages. However, that should not keep you from learning the languages superficially. And you can do that easily.

Get a 45-minute Berlitz (*http://www.berlitz.us*) tourist's audio language tape (or CD) in a bookstore and play it over and over again in your car. When you have listened to it about 30 times, you will be fluent in a couple of hundred words. You will be surprised how far you can get on such a vocabulary, and at the least, you will impress your local business contacts. You won't find it difficult in many places to do business in English, but that doesn't mean developing a few hundred words of the native language won't help you cement good relationships locally.

## Culture and Business Culture

Learning about the culture of another country is one of the joys of traveling, and it works just as well for business as for a tourist visit. But there is a business side to culture too. Call it business culture. It's something you should learn at home before dealing with people from any country and should certainly learn before visiting a country. Fortunately, there are excellent resources available.

The World Trade Press (*http://worldtradepress.com*) sells its *Passport* series. It offers about two dozen books, each on a different country. Each book contains a uniform set of about two dozen topics which cover the following:

- Greetings and courtesies
- Cultural stereotypes
- Work environment
- Making connections
- Negotiating tactics
- Business meetings
- Customs
- Dress and appearance
- Entertaining
- Socializing

You can use these at home, and it's a good idea to take them with you when you travel. They're priced at a modest $7 each.

If you're looking for one volume, try the World Trade Press *Global Road Warrior* Third Edition. It rolls the business information on 95 countries into 864 pages for a price of $65.

The World Trade Press *Country Business Guide* series covers about a dozen coutries in depth. Each book is an encyclopedia of doing business in a specific country. These books are not specifically directed at travel, but they contain useful information that you can use during your visit. Again, each book has a common set of about two dozen key business topics. These are priced at $25 each.

Another book not necessarily intended for travel but which contains comprehensive information on about 100 countries is the World Trade Press *World Trade Almanac 1996-1997* for $87. If you don't have anything else, this will get you off to a good start. Joe bought a used copy of this for $20 on eBay.

Finally, you can subscribe to the World Trade Reference (*http://worldtraderef.com*) where much of the import-export information developed by Word Trade Press is available and up-to-date.

Rand McNally (*http://randmcnally.com*) has about ten travel bookstores around the US that are packed full of useful travel books, some published by Rand McNally but most published by other publishers. You can also find maps and useful travelers' aids on its website.

World Trade Press and Rand McNally are not the only publishers covering business travel abroad. Look for other business travel books in major bookstores. Even the general travel books that contain cultural information—readily available in every bookstore—are better than nothing.

Take a look at *Kiss, Bow, or Shake Hands: How to Do Business in Sixty Countries*, Morrison et al, Adams Media, 1995, $20, and *Dun & Brad-*

*street's Guide to Doing Business Around the World*, Morrison et al, Printice Hall, 1996, $34, which together give you both cultural and business information.

### No Disaster

Learning the culture and business culture before your visit will probably not prevent you from making some stupid mistakes out of ignorance, but it will probably prevent your visit from becoming a horrid and unsalvageable disaster.

WorldBiz.com (*http://www.worldbiz.com*) offers a wide selection of reports on a huge number of countries. These are not the least expensive ones available, but they cover a lot of ground. If you can't find it elsewhere, this website is a good place to look.

For free information go to Executive Planet's International Business Culture and Etiquette (*http://www.executiveplanet.com*) a very useful website for understanding the business cultures of over three dozen countries. Also try the Export.com Trade Information Center (*http://web.ita.doc.gov/ticwebsite/tic.nsf/AF34FA880278BDD58525690D00656C6F/3B884AC0FF87831F85256926005340B3?*) for business information on various countries including some information on business travel and etiquette. The Foreign Agriculture Service (http://www.fas.usda.gov) of the US Department of Argiculture provides plenty of information on countries abroad, albeit with an argiculture flavor. To find cultural information, you will have to dig deep into the website. But it's there.

Don't miss Michigan State University's excellent Global Edge website (*http://globaledge.msu.edu*), which provides a wealth of information on countries abroad. It even offers an great online version of Global Warrior cited above for a low subscription rate.

Why is culture so important? Because it's different everywhere. Just the act of handshaking is different in different areas of the world. In the US it's strong and firm. In the Middle East it's limp. A gesture with the thumb and the index finger forming an O in the US means OK. In many places abroad it's an obscene gesture. You don't have to learn how to bow to the queen when you go to England, because you're unlikely to meet her. But you do have to learn how to bow when you go to Japan, because that's an ordinary courtesy everyone uses. You must eat with the fingers of your right hand when in the Middle East, because the left hand is used for tending to bodily functions. And on and on. Read *Gestures: Dos & Taboos of Body Language Around the World*, Roger E. Axtell, Wiley, New York, 1997.

## Activities

Traveling abroad for business is normally expensive. This is not a grassroots trip where you stay in quaint quarters, get off the beaten track, eat in pedestrian native restaurants, and camp on the beach. This is a business trip. It's going to be expensive, and you need to plan well to make the most of your time and money.

Plan and schedule your activities well ahead of time. Stay long enough to get the job done. Don't put all your eggs in one basket. That is, don't just meet with the people you do business with. Make other contacts to develop backup business relationships that you may have to use someday, perhaps sooner than you think.

Keep careful track of everyone you meet. Make sure you have all contact information (i.e., a business card). If nothing else, write notes on the back of each person's business cards to remind you of the people you meet.

When you plan to negotiate with people, having the latest draft of an agreement with you and using it in face-to-face negotiations will likely move things along faster.

A well organized trip is a productive trip. And a productive trip is likely to mean expanded sales when you return home. And don't forget to take your own cards with you. Lots of business cards.

## Customs Brokers and Freight Forwarders

Remembering Chapter 8, if your customs brokerage and freight forwarding relationships are in the country you're visiting, take the opportunity to drop in and meet them in person. If you are looking for such services, this is a good opportunity to make contact, evaluate, and negotiate.

## US Government

Don't miss the US Consulate when traveling abroad. It's there for specific reasons, and one of the primary reasons is to encourage trade with the US. It's your tax dollars at work. Take advantage of it. Stop in and chat with a consular officer. Find out what support you can expect from the consulate as you import or export in that country. When you get home and have a problem, it's helpful to be able to call someone that you've met face to face. And if you have a business problem while in country, the US Consulate is a good place to get help. In addition, the consulate may have information resources you can use while you're away from home.

The US Consulate is not the only place to get governmental support. Contact the US Commercial Service ahead of time for help, such as making the proper contacts when you visit. Then visit the US Commercial Service office when you arrive in the country. The only *raison d'etre* for the US Commercial Service is to help US businesses export abroad.

See Chapter 6 for links to websites such as Export.gov and Buy-USA.com that offer lists of the office locations in many countries that have US consultates and US Commercial Service offices.

## Industry

World Trade Centers (*http://iserve.wtca.org*) are another place to visit abroad. They are worldwide. Membership is the price you pay to use this commercial resource. Join in your locale.

And don't overlook American chambers of commerce abroad (*http://www.uschamber.com/international/default*). There may be an office in one of the cities you visit. Stop in and see how they can help you. It doesn't hurt to be a member too.

UPS provides a list of import-export shippers by continent on its website at *http://www.ups.com/content/corp/index.jsx* in the menu in the upper left corner. That will inform you of shipping people you can contact both before your travels and during your travels. Look for similar lists posted by other couriers.

## Where?

Because travel abroad is normally expensive and working in a country goes slow, don't try and do the entire world at once. It's better to take your best shot and do it right. That is, it's better to pick two countries and spend weeks in each rather than to pick ten countries and spend two or three days in each. Naturally, you will want to visit the countries where you have solid sales already or from which you already import products that sell well. Develop a solid basis in several countries and then expand later.

## Who?

Who are you looking for? Although the direct approach for import-export for eBay businesses is the least costly, you may find indirect sources that can help you build a profitable business too.

Let's take a look at direct sources for buying goods locally in a country abroad:

- Manufacturers

- Wholesalers

- Distributors

- Retailers (in some circumstances)

Direct sources for selling goods locally in a country abroad include:

- Distributors

- Retailers

- And, of course, an eBay marketplace abroad

Indirect sources are, in effect, middlemen that stand between you and direct sources (see Chapter 25). They can save you time and money, but they cost money too. The only way you can tell if they can help you to be more profitable is to evaluate what services they offer at what price. Here are some possibilities:

**Jobbers and Brokers** You sell or buy from a firm that sells or buys goods for you. These firms provide limited services.

**Manufacturers' Representatives** You buy from a firm that represents a manufacturer abroad. You will find such a firm in the US. You sell through a firm abroad that represents you. You will find such a firm abroad. Unless you are a manufacturer, seeking out such a representative abroad is probably not for you.

**Export Agents** These are firms that provide a broad range of services either for buying or selling. An Export Management Company (EMC) is a good example.

**Export Trading Companies** These are larger companies that handle large ongoing buying and selling relationships and do even more of the import-export work than export agents.

**Joint Venturers** A person or company that joint ventures with you is normally one that provides you exactly what you need (see Chapter 25).

As you can see, the plot thickens. Visiting a country abroad may not be just a three-day fling to visit a few wholesalers, a few government offices, and a few shippers. It's your opportunity to explore a broader business landscape.

# Shopping

All this talk about setting up business meetings and making new business contacts is great, especially for eBay businesses that are looking for manufacturers, wholesalers, joint venturers, and the like. But if you're a retailer looking for new products to sell—go shopping!

Buyers for the small boutique import shops and the big import retail chains (e.g., Pier One) shop all over the world looking for new products to be imported from abroad to sell in the US. This is a primary reason for traveling. Take your spouse and your kids and have them shop too. You don't have to be an eBay entrepreneur to spot cool new merchandise that isn't readily available in the US.

### More Tax Write-Offs

If your spouse and your kids shop for new products for your business, can you write off their travel expenses on your income tax too? In our opinion, it's not a stretch. But consult your accountant.

Shopping is the easy part. Once you've identified a few products you think you can import to the US and sell profitably, you have to make purchase arrangements. You have to find a reliable supply of the products at a price that makes sense. And you have to research compliance (with US Customs regulations).

Shopping, finding suppliers, and researching compliance can take time, plenty of time. That's why it's important to plan your visit (budget your time) to a country carefully.

# Summary

The best way to solidify a good trade relationship with a country abroad is to visit it. Be sure to learn the cultural byways before you go and master at least a superficial fluency in the language. Plan your trip well to take advantage of the opportunities to establish new relationships and bolster old ones with a broad range of governmental and commercial offices.

If you're traveling to find inventory, you're on the right track. Shop, shop, shop til you drop. Then find some reliable suppliers.

# *25*

## *Cross-Border Relationships*

The idea behind cross-border relationships is that someone in the other country will do the work that you would do if you could be there to establish a presence there. A whole range of local businesses can accommodate you for small-scale importing or exporting. For larger scale trade, you might want to have a partner or joint venturer instead. The ultimate is to open an office in a country abroad and staff it with your own employees. However, that requires a scale of operation that is unlikely for most eBay small businesses and therefore is beyond the scope of this book. Consequently this chapter will concentrate on local businesses and joint venturers.

# Services

Until the volume of your exports or imports from a particular country rises to a certain level, you don't need a cross-border relationship. You just need services. The service might be a customs broker, a freight forwarder, a wholesaler, or a manufacturer. In fact, you might be wise to shop around. Try different customs brokers, for example, to determine which gives a small business like yours the best service.

As your business grows with that particular country, however, you will need ongoing reliable services. That is the time to establish a good relationship with one local business, such as one customs broker. Theoretically, dealing with only one business will get you better service.

Import-export service companies have existed for a long time in the import-export business under such names as: manufacturer's representatives, export agents, and export trading companies (see Chapter 24). They will also start to provide services for eBay businesses as eBay becomes an entrenched international marketplace for international consumer commerce.

There may come a time, however, if your business expands, when you start to question whether you can't get the services you need less expensively. In fact, if you start out with a high volume of import-export business in a particular country, you may want to avoid excessive fees from the outset. That's where having a joint venturer comes in handy.

# Joint Ventures

In US law in most states there is little distinction between a joint venture and a partnership. Using the word *partnership* to describe a relationship implies an ongoing permanent relationship that includes all business activities. Using the words *joint venture* to describe a relationship implies a temporary relationship for a limited purpose that does not include all business activities.

Another way of expressing this idea is that a joint venture can last for 30 years, but many partnerships last forever. In any event, the law does not necessarily distinguish between the two ideas and generally treats them as one idea.

Suppose you are a small eBay business with a need to handle a heavy volume of either import or export business in Brazil. You can't afford to send an employee there. You're not quite sure how to handle the manufacturers there for your import business (into the US) or the eBay marketing and subsequent Mercado Libre sales for your export business (to Brazil). The freight forwarders and customs brokers may not be able to provide you with all the services you need.

## Import

The freight forwarders and customs brokers will handle your products in Brazil that you wish to ship from Brazil, import into the US, and eventually sell on eBay. But who will find the products? And who will find yet additional products later? Who will find the wholesalers and manufacturers and negotiate with them? Who will inspect the goods for quality? Who will research the reliability and trustworthiness of the sources of products? Who will establish the local banking relationships?

The answer can be a joint venturer in Brazil. This would be a person in Brazil with whom you make an agreement to carry through certain functions of the purchasing and shipping processes. You are partners with this person, not in all your business endeavors, but just in that part of your business activities that handles importing from Brazil.

Usually under a partnership (joint venture) agreement, the parties divide the profits, but not necessarily evenly. You can really make the partnership (joint venture) agreement almost anything you want it to be. The idea here is that the guy in Brazil is more than an employee or agent. He has a stake in the business.

From one point of view, this is an inexpensive way to use other people in your business. They don't get paid unless they perform and facilitate the generation of revenue. From another point of view, it's an expensive way to use other people in your business. They get a share of the profits. As the business grows and the profits grow, they get more and more money. At some point in the future, it becomes less expensive to have employees do the job instead.

## Export

The freight forwarders and customs brokers will handle your products in Brazil that you wish to export from the US, import into Brazil, and eventually sell on eBay US or Mercado Libre. They can even store the products for you in either bonded or cross-border warehouses (see Chapter 27). Some can even provide fulfillment services (shipping to individual consumers).

If you are selling on eBay US, this may be all you need. But you will depend on English-speaking consumers in a huge country that speaks Portuguese. Why not sell on Mercado Libre too? Or, perhaps you should sell on Mercado Libre instead?

If you sell on Mercado Libre, who is going to manage the marketing and sales effort? Who is going to translate the product information, specifications, and promotional materials into Portuguese? Who is going to create the Mercado Libre ads and enter them on Mercado Libre? Who is going to handle payments in Reals, the Brazilian currency? Who is going to handle customer service, your most important product?

Again, the answer can be a joint venturer in Brazil. This would be a person in Brazil with whom you make an agreement to carry on many of these business activities.

## Companies

A joint venturer doesn't have to be a person. It can be a company. Your interest is in carrying on certain business activities and getting certain tasks completed in order to make your eBay business work in Brazil. If you can cost-effectively joint venture with a Brazilian company instead of an individual, that may be more secure than a business relationship with an individual.

# Finding Joint Venturers

Finding partners for your activities in countries abroad is not easy, just like finding business partners at home is not so easy. You have to talk with a lot of potential partners before finding a fit. But conducting business with a joint venturer in another country is not unusual.

## Where to Look

Here are some places where you can find potential joint venturers.

- Government directories
- Commercial directories
- Website directories
- Industry and professional organizations
- Industry trade centers
- Industry trade shows
- Import-export (trade) shows
- Import-export (trade) centers
- Other entrepreneurs doing business on eBay US

- Other entrepreneurs doing business on eBays abroad

- Online communities such as eBay Discussion Boards

- Import-export conferences and seminars

As you can see from the list above, finding prospects to be your joint venturer in another country will probably be easy for you, even though narrowing the prospects down to one partner takes longer.

At BookCenter.com (*http://bookcenter.com*), you will find a link to TradeAffiliates.com (*http://tradeaffiliates.com*) where you can potentially find a PayPal member in another country with whom you can establish a joint venture.

BuyUSA.com (*http://www.buyusa.com*) is a major website run by the US Department of Commerce for exporters. It has a directory that enables you to search for potential partners abroad. Business people abroad can also search for partners inside the US.

## *Why Joint Venturers?*

Most import-export books will advise you to seek joint venturers only after you have grown large and successful. Until then, they would have you believe, you are better off hiring services to get things done in countries abroad. And there may be some truth in their advice. Certainly every business is different, and you should explore all the possibilities to determine which is the most cost-effective for you.

Nonetheless, we like the joint-venture concept. It has advantages for all sizes of import-export businesses. A good strategy is to find someone just like you with whom to joint venture. For instance, if you are a one-person business or a small partnership dealing in clothing, find a joint venturer abroad that's a one-person business or small partnership dealing in clothing. You are more likely to form a joint venture with such a small business abroad than you are with a larger bureaucratic corporation abroad.

When you partner with a business abroad, the partnership is typically not a general one. It's limited to the joint business activities with some provision for covering joint expenses and sharing in the profits of the joint venture activities. Each business—yours and the business abroad—covers its own general business expenses and expenses for doing other business that has nothing to do with the joint venture. Consequently, finding a joint venturer can be almost like getting a branch office in a country abroad for next to nothing. (Ultimately, it doesn't come cheap, since joint venturers share in the profits.) The start-up costs are low because the other business is paying its own way and is established in the target country.

Thus, we like the joint venture idea where:

> You are doing (or will do) a substantial amount of volume in a particular country;

> You expect the volume to grow or at least continue for a signifcant time into the future; and

> You don't have the capital to pay fees for services during start-up.

As you can see, a joint venture is not just a strategy for mature businesses, it can work well for start-ups too. And we know of such joint ventures that work well.

# US Consulate

The US Consulate isn't going to be your joint venturer, but you can still have a relationship. If you get a chance to travel abroad, go out of your way to meet a consular officer at the US Consulate. See Chapter 24. Not only can you get information you may need during your visit but you will have someone to call when you get home and need additional information.

## Summary

In the import-export business, you need cross-border relatonships. The only question is, what kind? Do you just need services? Or, do you need more? Can you pay fees cost-effectively, or is a joint venture something you should consider? Each business is different, and each will come to its own conclusion. There is no one-size-fits-all solution.

The point to this chapter is for you to devote some time to considering what kind of cross-border relationships you need and then taking action to establish them.

# VII

## Special Ventures

# *26*

## *Manufacturing Abroad*

Have something made for you abroad to sell on eBay US? Sounds like a terrible idea, doesn't it? Why? Well, in the US things manufactured in small quantities in small factories are often expensive, and it's difficult to find a way to make a profit selling such custom-made items on eBay. In the US, we tend to think that products must be produced in great numbers in big factories in order to be saleable and profitable.

But things are different abroad. The price of labor is lower. Nonetheless, in many countries there are pools of skilled craftsmen capable of inexpensively manufacturing a wide range of high-quality items. This presents an opportunity for you to actually have items made abroad in reasonably small quantities that you think will be big sellers on eBay US after you import them.

# How To?

OK, if this is a good idea, how do you do it? The best answer is, you have to be there. How do you go there? You go there with a plan of how you're going work intensely for a number of days or weeks to make contacts with small manufacturers, visit their factories, and examine the quality of their products. Sure, you can probably make arrangements with visiting manufacturers at trade shows or meetings in the US, but nothing beats going there—wherever "there" happens to be. You will find many more potential manufacturers in the locale (e.g., Hong Kong) than you will find at trade shows in the US.

As tourists, we have had items inexpensively manufactured for us abroad in small factories and back-of-the-house workshops. If it makes sense for tourists to have things custom manufactured abroad inexpensively, it surely makes sense for eBay retailers.

Does this idea work for everything? Surely not. First, you have to evaluate your product.

Is it the type of product that can be made less expensively abroad somewhere?

Is it a hand-crafted item made with low tech tools, or is it a high tech item that requires a high level of specialized manufacturing capability?

Does the target country have the manufacturing capabilities you need?

How much competition is there between factories in the country?

How can the product be shipped?

Then you have to evaluate the profitability.

Is the sale of the product potentially profitable in the US after shipping costs and import duties?

You will find many factories abroad quite eager to get your business. When you find some likely candidates to do your manufacturing, you need to further evaluate them.

Does the factory have the quality control necessary to manufacture a marketable product for you?

Does the factory have a reliable source of raw materials?

Can the manufacturing be scaled up if your eBay sales effort is successful?

Do the factory personnel speak English?

As they say, "This is not rocket science." It's quite easy to make manufacturing arrangements abroad. But it helps to go there to get the ball rolling.

# Template Products

The section above assumes that you design the product, set the specifications, and seek a manufacturer that can produce the product for you. However, that's not necessarily the typical case. A more typical case might be dealing with a manufacturer that offers a product close to what you want that can be modified to your specifications. This might be called a template product. The manufacturer provides the template, and you fill it in with your unique but superficial design.

For example, suppose you want to manufacture and sell a digital timer with a alphanumeric display programmed specifically to time the cooking of French food. You find a manufacturer in Taipei that makes digital timers similar to what you seek. You find that such timers can be easily programmed for your purpose. Consequently, you make a deal to have the manufacturer design a special plastic case with your logo in which to house the preexisting product (the digital timer) specifically programmed for your purpose. You have created a unique, useful, and inexpensive product without starting from scratch.

Making your product from a template product can be as simple as just having your logo put on it or as complex as having a host of extra parts added as well as waterproofing it. This is a particularly appropriate means of manufacturing complex new products that are similar to unbranded existing products.

You might note that you are more likely to be able to order a template product at a trade show in the US that includes foreign exhibitors than to order a custom-made product.

# Crafts

One of the great delights of traveling abroad is discovering the local crafts. Often you can find unique items that you think will sell well in the US but are not yet readily available in the US. This presents an opportunity.

First, you have to look upon craft items as manufactured products, even if they aren't made in a factory. You have to ask all the same questions (outlined above). For instance, if you are going to sell a steady stream of craft products, you have to be assured of an ongoing, reliable, high-quality supply.

Second, you have to find craftsmen who will tailor their products to your designs and specifications, and you have to find them in sufficient numbers to produce enough for your sales goals.

Producing crafts locally can be similar to manufacturing goods locally. Look upon it as dealing with a decentralized factory.

### Designs and Specifications

When you find a craft item you desire to import and sell, in many instances you may have to alter the design and specifications to make it a commercially acceptable (or reliably functional) product in the US or other countries. Taking a custom manufacturing approach makes sense.

On the other hand, the charm of many craft items is that they are closer to art and have limited functionally compared to less aesthetically pleasing craft items that are fully functional. For these charming items, the custom manufacturing approach is undesirable. They are what they are and do not need customization.

# VAT

Don't forget the value-added taxes (VAT) that many countries abroad have. Will you have to pay the VAT on the items you arrange to have manufactured and exported? If so, how soon can you get a refund on the VAT? Setting up your procedures and follow-up to get refunds on your VAT in a timely manner will help prevent cash-flow problems.

# At Home

Don't get us wrong. We are not advocating that you run off to some country abroad to have your product ideas manufactured without checking at home first. Put in some research regarding manufacturing in the US first. Not everything is less expensive to manufacture abroad. And manufacturing abroad can not always provide the quality you need for your particular products. It would be very embarassing to find that you can get an product made for $24.37 US in Baltimore when you've been paying $32.79 US (plus shipping) to have it made in Yokohama with less quality. Manufacturing abroad is a great opportunity for eBay retailers, but it's not the answer for every product and every situation.

# Summary

Should you decide to have products manufactured for you in a country abroad, you will follow a long business tradition. It must be a good idea, because many American businesses have done it and many still do it. It's a substantial opportunity that may be very profitable for you to explore.

Check out custom manufacturing opportunities at home first. If that doesn't pan out, take your product ideas on the road abroad.

# 27

## *Warehousing*

Warehousing abroad is a technique already in use by many eBay businesses. It is really both a cost-savings technique and a customer service technique. It can save you time, energy, and paperwork in countries where you sell a reasonable volume of identical products. The technique is essentially importing products in bulk into the country where the products will be sold and delivered, storing them, and then shipping each product individually. Because the freight forwarders and customs brokers are also in the business of warehousing, even a small business or an eBay business can have a cross-border or bonded ware-housing program at a reasonable price.

# The Normal Way

The normal way to sell abroad from eBay US is to send the item via the Postal Service or a courier (e.g., FedEx). It is up to you to provide accurate and appropriate documentation (e.g., commercial invoice, certificate of origin). It is up to the buyer to clear customs. That is, it's up to the buyer to pay duties, VAT, sales tax, and excise tax, if required, and otherwise hire a firm, such as a customs broker, to do the necessary tasks for clearance. This is a lot of responsibility, both bureaucratic and financial, to put on a buyer.

Likewise, if you sell products on an eBay abroad, you still normally deliver an item the same way. You still have to export the item from the US, and the buyer has to import it into his country.

# The Smart Way

The normal way is OK for small volumes of identical products sold in one country. However, when the volume grows, or for more expensive low-volume items, you will want to consider a smarter way to do your fulfillment. The smart way assumes a few things. First, the products to be sold within a reasonable time are identical. For instance, if you sell one Model 550 XTG ionic air purifier (weight 3.1 pounds) a year, three Model 660 XTRs (weight 3.7 pounds) a year , and two Model 880 XTWs (weight 4.6 pounds) a year in Belgium with price range of $185 to $325, you don't need to warehouse them abroad. Just send them via a courier.

If you sell 20 Model 770 XTM ionic air purifiers (weight 2.9 pounds - price $135) a month, you might be a candidate for cross-border ware-housing.

If you also sell 6 Model 38RG commercial air conditioners (weight 242 pounds) a year at $5,600 each, you might be a candidate for a bonded warehouse.

# Export and Store

You can export and store the goods in the destination country before they are sold. To do so you can use cross-border warehousing or bonded warehousing.

## Cross-Border Warehouse

The Model 770 XTM example (20 sales a month) is simply the process of exporting a product to a country abroad. Instead of the buyer having the responsibility to import it, however, you as the seller take that responsibility yourself. In the case of Belgium, you export the products from the US, import them into Belgium by clearing customs there, and store them in a warehouse in Belgium. The warehouse then fulfills the orders as you sell the products either from eBay US or from eBay Belgium. This is called cross-border warehousing.

Note that in cross-border warehousing, you pay the duties and taxes as you import the items and then warehouse them. You pass your costs on to the buyer one way or another.

In Canada, cross-border warehousing is done through a special Non-Resident Importer (NRI) process, which is ideal for many US eBay businesses (go to *http://aacb.com/imex/canada.htm#nri* for more information).

## Bonded Warehouse

The Model 38RG example (6 sales a year) is the process of exporting an expensive product with occasional sales to a country abroad. Because the products are not yet sold, you put them into a bonded warehouse. Until you sell an item, you don't have to pay duties and taxes on it. Once you sell one item, you pay the duties and taxes, clear customs, and it moves out of the bonded warehouse.

### Bonding

The act of bonding is simply segregating the bonded section of a warehouse from the remaining space. All goods that go into and out of a bonded warehouse (or a bonded section) are accounted for to customs. In fact, customs conducts surprise audits of the goods in bonded warehouses to make sure there's no cheating.

## Which Is for What?

You can see from the examples that cross-border warehousing is for low-price volume sales items. You sell so many so often that it would be costly and inefficient to clear them through customs individually.

Bonded warehousing is for higher price low-volume items. It would impair your cash flow to clear them through customs prematurely. So, you clear them individually as you sell them.

Keep in mind that an important part of using warehousing can be lower cost shipping and greater convenience. For instance, if you can ship Model 770 XTMs in bulk via surface transportation instead of via courier, you can gain a significant savings. Likewise, if you can reduce the shipping time for Model 38RG, which has to be shipped via surface shipping, you can provide convenience. By shipping to a warehouse and then shipping to buyers as sales are made, you reduce the shipping time, in effect, to the buyers.

Indeed, the point here is customer service. The customer buys, and you deliver immediately without hassles, even though the product travels from the US to the country where the customer resides.

## Store and Import

Another case is simply importing a product into your country from a country abroad, let's say from Singapore to the US. You buy directly from the factory in Singapore and import the products to your warehouse in the US. Nothing unusual about that. But what if you sell the products in Singapore via eBay as well as the US? You may have to ship the products back to Singapore one at a time. In this case, it makes sense to leave some of the products in a warehouse in Singapore. It needs to be a warehouse that offers fulfillment services. This makes a lot of sense. Why import from Singapore to the US, just to ship back to Singapore?

## Benefits to You

You reduce your bureaucratic workload. When you move products across borders in bulk, you do the paperwork once for all the products instead of one product at a time. In doing so, you are able to provide great customer service. You ship in the country where the buyer is located. This benefits your customers considerably.

## Benefits to Your Customers

When you ship in the country where the buyer is located, it's much like shipping in your own country. You provide the following benefits to customers:

- No clearance hassle

- Reduced clearance and transportation cost per item

- Faster delivery time

- No surprises

Although the buyer pays a higher purchase price because you've paid the clearance and shipping expenses already, the costs are more certain, too, because the costs have been paid. And the costs per item are lower. It's just a much cleaner process from the buyer's point of view. And it's great customer service.

### For Example, US Exporting and Cross-Border Warehousing

For the European market you can warehouse in one port (e.g., Rotterdam) and then ship to all the European Common Market countries. For Canada, you can warehouse in a Canadian city and ship to all of Canada, the greatest trade partner of the US.

# Finding a Warehouse

You have two problems with cross-border and bonded warehousing. First, you need to find a warehouse that will store your products securely and inexpensively. Second, you have to find one that offers fulfillment services. And most readers will have to do that in Belgium or Singapore while sitting at a desk in the US. What do you do?

It all goes back to customs brokerage and freight forwarding. As we said earlier in the book, customs brokers have become freight forwarders, and freight forwarders have become customs brokers. And both now offer cross-border and bonded warehouses in many places. That is, they provide inexpensive warehousing that even eBay businesses can afford, and they will do your fulfillment for you.

Computers have been a boon to the cross-border warehousing business. You export to a country abroad with a bulk shipment. Your full-service customs broker (or freight forwarder) clears customs for you, pays all taxes and duties, charges your account, and stores the products in its cross-border or bonded warehouse. Then all you have to do is put in an order via the Internet, and the warehouse ships an item to a buyer in the country abroad. Slick!

## Summary

Keep in mind that cross-border and bonded warehousing works best for multiple identical products to be sold in one country abroad. It doesn't work for all products, but if you need it, you can get it from your freight forwarder or customs broker. There are plenty of small eBay businesses using this technique, so it's not just something for the big retailers.

# *28*

## *Services and Digital Content*

Here in the US we hear a lot about service jobs going abroad. For instance, Silicon Valley software companies hire programmers in India, Russia, and other places where the work force is skilled in programming. That's a two-way street, however, and many American companies and individuals provide skilled services abroad. What makes this all possible? The Internet!

The Internet provides inexpensive, reliable, and quick communication and the capability to efficiently carry huge amounts of multimedia information (e.g., text, images, audio, video). So, of course, we're talking about intellectual and bureaucratic services, not physical services.; that is, white-collar sevices, not blue-collar services.

### Blue-Collar Services

Although this chapter focuses on white-collar services delivered over the Internet, blue-collar services are not beyond the realm of possibility internationally. For instance, Bechtel in San Francisco, a worldwide contractor for huge construction projects, provides a host of white-collar services including design, project management, logistics control, and the like. It hires blue-collar workers in the locale of the project. Nonetheless, certain skilled blue-collar workers who cannot be found in the locale must be brought in from elsewhere for the duration of the project. That demonstrates that if you are a skilled blue-collar worker or head a team of skilled workers, there may be project work waiting for you abroad with foreign companies or foreign governments. eBay advertising internationally may be a way to put your name in front of foreign project managers cost-effectively.

When you think about it, you realize you can easily set up a virtual workplace on the Internet where people from different physical locations can collaborate electronically in one place online. Much of the basic software (e.g., Microsoft Word) supports collaboration, and specialty collaboration software is readily available too. The only thing missing is meetings. (And that may be a good thing!) In any event, you can even have online conferences, which can substitute for face-to-face meetings. In the future, people will start to use video conferencing via the Web more and more, perhaps a reasonable substitute for face-to-face meetings.

### Do You Need Collaboration Software?

Plenty of fancy collaboration software is available. Some is inexpensive and some quite expensive. But do you really need it? Email provides an excellent collaboration medium. You can easily communicate and also transfer files that contain a broad range of work product—from Excel spreadsheets to color images.

Finally, don't forget voice over IP (VoIP) telephone (see Chapter 23). That's telephone over the Internet. It works well. Why VoIP rather than the regular telephone? Internationally, it's much less expensive. For instance, Vonage (*http://www.vonage.com*) charges 4 cents a minute from the US to Singapore. That's less than a local call across the San Francisco Bay Area.

But what about digital content (intellectual property)? Isn't that just like services in that you can transport such content anywhere via the Internet? For instance, you can attach a digital photograph to an email message and send it anywhere.

# Services

Is selling services on eBay fact or fantasy? It turns out to be a little of both. This is an opportunity to get in on the ground floor, and the demand is not limited to just the US.

### Employee Discretion

US corporations are finding it's more cost-efficient to give employees discretion to buy supplies and equipment and to hire outside contractors, within certain cost limits, than to control such expenditures through the purchasing department or the contracting department. Consequently, skilled individuals are actually contracting for work on small projects with corporations usually dealing directly with the employees responsible for such projects.

Certain industries do a huge amount of contracting with individuals. For instance, publishers, including huge publishing corporations, contract with individuals to do editing, copy editing, art work, and typography, thus providing thousands of self-employed individuals ongoing work. And that even includes authors, the indentured servants of the publishing industry.

Certainly, there are opportunities for skilled people to sell their services in their own country and in other countries as well. Americans have a wide range of technical skills that are needed in other countries. Individuals can provide those skills perhaps more cost-effectively for users (buyers) abroad than other means of providing them.

eBay appears to be the logical marketplace for services to be advertised and procured both domestically and internationally, and eBay is conscious of this and is working to make it more feasible.

## Import-Export

There are opportunities here going in both directions. US technology is in high demand worldwide whether it be entertainment, website technology, oil drilling, or water treatment. Likewise, many countries abroad can provide specialized skills or low-cost intellectual and bureaucratic labor.

Services are like any other product. They can be bought at wholesale and sold at retail. We call that "brokering" services.

Joe has been contacted several times by such a broker who was attempting to sell bookkeeping services done by personnel outside the US. This is significant, because this is really getting down to the grass roots. When you try to sell an author bookkeeping services, you've reached the bottom of the food chain. This clearly indicates that importing and exporting services is not limited to big companies.

## Services on eBay

In *eBay the Smart Way* and *eBay Business the Smart Way*, Joe speculates at length about how services might be sold on eBay. Elance, which provides a marketplace for selling services online, has enjoyed a special status on eBay going back almost to the beginning. Meg Whitman, the CEO of eBay, announced at the 2003 eBay conference that eBay will attempt in the future to find a way for people to sell their services more easily and efficiently on eBay.

As you may suspect from reading this section, this aspect of online commerce is for pioneers. No one has quite figured out how to do it well yet. Elance, although successful, has never had the wild growth rate of eBay itself. Selling services on eBay is a wide-open opportunity.

## Compliance

What about compliance with governmental restrictions (i.e., customs)? This is a tough question. Is anyone going to pay any attention to it? The fact is that people can pass intellectual and bureaucratic services back and forth across national borders on the Internet with impunity, even if there are any governmental restrictions on services in a particular country. Naturally, there are people who will voluntarily comply with governmental restrictions even if there is no chance of getting caught for ignoring such restrictions. But will anyone even ask about restrictions? It's unlikely. Most people will just use email to provide their services anywhere in the world that they can find customers and clients.

### If You're Big

You have to worry about compliance when you operate a medium or large firm that constantly provides services across borders. The bigger you are, the more likely it will be that someone in governmental authority will notice what you're doing. If there is compliance to be done, you will be well advised to find out what it is and do it.

You do need to pay special attention to prohibited exports or imports, particularly when related to national defense, public health, or public welfare. For example, it's illegal to export encryption technology (e.g., encryption consulting) from the US to another country, and you can get yourself into grave trouble for doing so. It's a national defense restriction, which the US government takes very seriously.

All things considered, however, it seems that you can provide services across borders without worrying about restrictions, duties, taxes or getting caught (if in violation of a restriction).

However, because this is a book about eBay, we are concerned here only about services marketed and sold on eBay. eBay is a public record which anyone—including customs officials—can read and save. Consequently, in dealing on eBay, you leave a record of what you've sold (or bought). That should give you pause when seeking to avoid restrictions, duties, and taxes that may apply to services.

# Digital Content

Content is another word for intellectual property, and intellectual property is a creation in a communications medium or in multimedia. For instance, a Disney movie, a Harry Potter novel, a Michael Jackson song, or a copy of Time magazine are all intellectual property—or what those in the digital world call "content."

Most content can be digitized and therefore easily transported via the Internet. For instance, a Harry Potter novel makes only a relatively small digital file, which can be attached to an email. A Michael Jackson song in MPEG form is also a relatively small digital file. A copy of Time magazine including images is also a convenient-size file to send over the Internet.

On the other hand, a Disney movie digitized is a huge file inconvenient to transport over the Internet, but that's not the whole story. What is inconvenience? With broadband, you can transport a Disney movie or multiple movies in a reasonably convenient manner, particularly if you do it as a background or overnight task on your computer.

## Compared to Services

Content is a mass product used by many people. It is usually in one medium (e.g., audio) or in one multimedia format (e.g., motion pictures and sound). As a mass product, it is likely to have governmental restrictions (e.g., a duty or tax).

In contrast, a service usually comprises a custom communication in random media. In one project, the services might be delivered by telephone, report (text), correspondence (text), and images (digital art or photographs). In another project another combination of media might be used. The communications are usually custom-made for the customer or client. The customer is not necessarily viewed as buying a *product*.

Thus, digital content in comparison to a service is more like a physical product. It is mass-produced (replicated) and distributed to multiple customers. What they both have in common is that they can easily pass through national borders without restrictions.

## Copyrights

You do have to pay attention to copyrights when selling content. If you violate a copyright by illicitly distributing content owned by someone else, you may not only violate the US copyright laws but also the copyright laws of the destination country. Content is protected worldwide by a web of international copyright treaties.

The other side of the issue is that you need to be careful when distributing digital content for which you have a copyright. How will you protect yourself against others infringing on your copyright in a worldwide digital market?

We, of course, do not advise you to violate the copyright laws of any country or violate the copyrights of any content creator. And we do advise you to do whatever you can to protect your own copyrights both in the US and worldwide. The only reason copyrights are mentioned here is that they are an important consideration in the world trade of intellectual property. They are protected by most countries. And copyright owners do have a financial incentive to go after infringers.

## Risk

What is your risk of getting caught for not paying duties or taxes or otherwise failing to comply with trade restrictions in regard to digital content? We will again remind you that in dealing on eBay, you leave a public record of what you've sold (or bought). Will customs officials someday be watching online marketplaces like eBay to spot potential violators?

# Summary

Services and digital content seem to travel across national borders outside the normal customs system. The risk of getting caught by customs in violation of whatever restrictions exist, if any, seems nil. This presents an opportunity for certain types of services and digital content businesses to thrive, although you are certainly best advised to comply with all appropriate national regulations. eBay is a marketplace where content can be sold through auctions and where services can be sold through auctions that are more like advertising than like product sales.

---

### End of the Book

---

You have reached the end of the book. We hope that you've found this book enjoyable and useful. And we wish you the best of luck in your global endeavors.

---

# Appendix I  Top 10 Tips for Selling to Consumers Abroad

**The top 10 tips for success on eBay US in selling to foreign consumers** follow below, not necessarily in order of priority:

1. **Advertise**  Indicate in your auction ad that you accept bidders (buyers) from other countries. If you don't accept bidders from all other countries, indicate the countries from which you will accept bidders.

2. **Keep It Simple**  Use simple language in your auction ad, and never use slang or abbreviations.

3. **Accept Various Payments**  Get set up to accept international payment as many ways as are practical and secure.

4. **Ship Various Ways**  Get set up to ship the most inexpensive way possible and also to ship in other ways that may be faster, more expensive, or more secure.

5. **Prepare Customs Documents**  Include the proper customs documents with your shipment (e.g., commercial invoice).

6. **Include Insurance**  Always include insurance as part of the shipping and handling. International shipping tends to be more risky.

7. **Use the Telephone**  Don't hesitate to use the telephone to resolve serious problems with bidders. Get an inexpensive voice-over-IP telephone service.

8. **Export in Bulk**  Consider becoming an exporter in bulk (see Appendix IV) for those countries in which you do a lot of business. Take advantage of cross-border warehousing.

9. **Prohibited**  Make sure your exports aren't on the US prohibited exports list.

10. **Establish a Trade Reference System**  Set up a trade reference system to put all necessary import-export information at your fingertips.

———

Selling to consumers abroad can increase your market considerably. Don't shy away from this great opportunity. Instead, go for it!

# *Appendix II  Top 9 Tips for Buying on eBays Abroad*

**The top 9 tips for buying items on foreign eBays** follow below, not necessarily in order of priority:

1. **Start with the Familiar**  To start, pick an eBay abroad with a foreign language that you know. Graduate later to other eBays for which you don't know the language.

2. **Use a Dictionary**  Get an inexpensive paperback language dictionary (e.g., English-Spanish) to find key words for searching.

3. **Translate**  Use Babel Fish or one of the other online automatic digital translators to read other-language eBay ads and communicate with the seller via email.

4. **Be Ready to Pay**  Pay careful attention to which payment methods the seller requires. Be ready to comply. But in any event, also ask to pay via PayPal.

5. **Understand the Currency**  Understand the national currency of the seller and, if necessary, use an online currency converter to understand the bidding and pricing.

6. **Be Aware of Time Zones**  Pay attention to the time zone differences. Keep them in mind when you need to communicate with the seller.

7. **Look at the Shipping Options**  Carefully evaluate the shipping options. Shipping can be expensive.

8. **For Sellers**  If you're a seller, foreign eBays are great places to find merchandise you can import to the US and sell on eBay US. In other words, shop.

9. **Have Fun!**  This is a great way to find unique and inexpensive (or expensive) merchandise. Loosen up and have some fun.

––––––––

Don't be afraid of buying on eBays abroad. There is plenty of great merchandise to purchase, much of it at prices well below what you will have to pay for it in the US. And it's not difficult to make a purchase. Try it!

# *Appendix III  Top 8 Tips for Importing to Sell on eBay*

**The top 8 tips for importing in bulk** to subsequently sell on eBay US follow below, not necessarily in order of priority:

1. **Find Reliable Suppliers**  Find suppliers you can rely on for the goods you want to import.

2. **Understand the Agreement**  Understand what your responsibilities and costs are under the purchase agreement, particularly in regard to

shipping and insurance. Sometimes it takes careful anaylsis to understand the shipping and insurance provisions.

3. **Use a Letter of Credit** Use contingent payments where appropriate. That means an escrow arrangement or—more likely—a letter of credit.

4. **Use PayPal** Experiment with paying via PayPal where possible.

5. **Employ a Customs Broker** Use a customs broker or freight forwarder in the US.

6. **Check Insurance Coverage** Don't overlook insurance for shipping for each leg and mode of transportation.

7. **Estimate the Cost** Estimate the US duties, excise tax (if any), shipping, insurance, and customs clearance fees prior to making a buying decision. Then add them to the purchase price in order to estimate your cost of goods.

8. **Minimize Your Currency Exchange Risk** Develop a strategy for minimizing your risk with currency exchange rates if making a delayed payment.

———

Buying abroad in bulk and importing to the US for subsequent sale on eBay US can be profitable. Give it a try while keeping the above tips in mind.

# Appendix IV  Top 7 Tips for Exporting to Countries Abroad

**The top 7 tips for exporting goods in bulk to foreign countries** to subsequently sell on eBay US or on foreign eBays follow below, not necessarily in order of priority:

1. **Estimate Costs**  Estimate duties, VAT, sales tax, excise tax, shipping, and insurance for a foreign country before you export a bulk shipment.

2. **Prepare Documents**  Make sure you prepare the necessary customs documents to accompany the bulk shipment.

3. **Employ a Freight Forwarder**  Use a freight forwarder or customs broker in the foreign country. Choose one that offers bonded and cross-border warehousing. You usually find a freight forwarder or customs broker in a foreign country through one with which you have a relationship in the US.

4. **Use Bonded Warehousing**  Consider bonded warehousing for large, heavy, and expensive items that that are occasionally sold.

5. **Use Cross-Border Warehousing**  Consider cross-border warehousing for inexpensive items that are routinely sold.

6. **Develop a Strategy**  Develop a strategy for marketing your merchandise on foreign eBays, particularly taking into account language differences.

7. **Joint Venturer**  Consider using a joint-venturer in the foreign country for supervising the importation of goods as well as marketing and selling on eBay in the foreign country.

---

Exporting in bulk for subsequent sales on eBay US or foreign eBays saves money for end-consumers on shipping, insurance, and customs clearance. Thereby, it helps you provide great customer service.

# *Appendix V  Foreign Countries*

The consular offices of foreign governments in the US exist in the US to help you do business with commercial enterprises in their countries and to help such commercial enterprises do business in the US. Although it's true they have other duties such as assisting their citizens inside the US, a primary reason for their existence is to encourage commerce. Thus, a consular office may be able to help you make your exports to a particular country go smoother by providing information on the customs regulations, duties, taxes, business practices, culture, language, and the like. The US State Department provides an up-to-date list of foreign consular offices at *http://www.state.gov/s/cpr/rls/fco*, which contains information on each office including telephone numbers and the names of personnel.

Below we provide a robust but incomplete list of countries to provide you with cryptic information on each that is likely to appear in documents, import-export publications, and governmental forms.

### Country

| Capital City | Dialing Code | Currency | Currency Code |
|---|---|---|---|
| Time (GMT) | 2-Letter Code | 3-Letter Code | Numeric Code |

### United States

| Washington | 1 | US Dollar | USD |
|---|---|---|---|
| -5 | US | USA | 840 |

### Latvia

| Riga | 371 | Lat | LVL |
|---|---|---|---|
| +2 | LV | LVA | 428 |

The Legend for each country is as follows:

**Capital City:** The capital city of the country, where you can usually find many information resources.

**Dialing Code:** The international telephone dialing code for the country. To dial a foreign country, you need the International Access Code (IAC) for your own country. For the US it is 011. Thus, to call Latvia from the US, you dial 011 first, 371 second, and the telephone number in Latvia third (including a Latvia area code).

**Currency:** The name of the national currency.

**Currency Code:** This is the ISO 4217 Alpha currency code. For the US Dollar it is USD. The ISO numeric currency code is usually the same as the ISO numeric country code (see below), unless the country shares a currency with several other countries (e.g., Euro). ISO is the acronym for International Organization for Standardization.

**Time:** The time is expressed as the time zone of the capital city. It's negative if west of Greenwich, England. (It's behind.) It's positive if east of Greenwich. (It's ahead.) The acronym GMT stands for Greenwich Mean Time. If you're not sure where a country is located, the time zone may help you locate it. For instance, Wellington New Zealand is +12, which puts it on the opposite of the globe from Greenwich.

### eBay Time

eBay time is Pacific Standard Time (PST) in the US. (eBay headquarters is in San Jose, California.) That's –8 GMT as expressed in this Appendix. So, if you want to know the eBay time east of Greenwich, you add the opposite-sign numbers (eBay time plus local time) as if there were no signs. For instance, for Riga, Latvia (+2 GMT), you add (8 + 2 = 10) to find Riga is 10 hours ahead of San Jose. However, to calculate the eBay time on the west side of Greenwich, you subtract like-sign numbers (eBay time minus local time) as if there were no signs. Thus, for the eBay time in Washington, DC (–5 GMT), you subtract (8 – 5 = 3) to find Washington is 3 hours ahead of San Jose.

Note that for the eBay time west of San Jose but east of the international date line in the middle of the Pacific, you will get a negative number when you do your calculations. For example, for Honolulu, Hawaii (–10 GMT), you subtract (8 – 10 = –2) to find that Honolulu is 2 hours behind San Jose.

**2-Letter Code:** This is the ISO 3166 2-letter code for the country. These codes are commonly used in communications.

**3-Letter Code:** This is the ISO 3166 3-letter code.

**Numeric Code:** This is the ISO 3166 numeric code.

A good place to find additional cryptic trade information on individual countries is the latest edition of *Dictionary of International Trade*, Edward G. Hinkelman, World Trade Press, Novato, California.

### Angola

| Luanda | 244 | Kwanza<br>New Kwanza | AOA<br>AON |
|--------|-----|----------------------|------------|
| +1 | AO | AGO | 24 |

### Argentina

| Buenos Aires | 54 | Argentinian Peso | ARS |
|--------------|----|------------------|-----|
| -3 | AR | ARG | 32 |

### Armenia

| Yerevan | 374 | Dram | AMD |
|---------|-----|------|-----|
| +3 | AM | ARM | 51 |

### Australia

| Canberra | 61 | Australian Dollar | AUD |
|----------|----|-------------------|-----|
| +10 | AU | AUS | 36 |

### Austria

| Vienna | 43 | Euro | EUR |
|--------|----|------|-----|
| +1 | AT | AUT | 40 |

### Azerbaijan

| Baku | 994 | Manat | AZM |
|------|-----|-------|-----|
| +3 | AZ | AZE | 31 |

## Bangladesh

| Dhaka | 880 | Taka | BDT |
|-------|-----|------|-----|
| +6 | BD | BGD | 50 |

## Belarus

| Mensk | 375 | Belarussian Ruble | BYB |
|-------|-----|-------------------|-----|
| +2 | BY | BLR | 112 |

## Belgium

| Brussels | 32 | Euro | EUR |
|----------|-----|------|-----|
| +1 | BE | BEL | 56 |

## Belize

| Belmopan | 501 | Belize Dollar | BZD |
|----------|-----|---------------|-----|
| -6 | BZ | BLZ | 84 |

## Bhutan

| Thimphu | 975 | Ngultrum | BTN |
|---------|-----|----------|-----|
| +6 | BT | BTN | 64 |

## Bolivia

| La Paz | 591 | Boliviano | BOB |
|--------|-----|-----------|-----|
| -4 | BO | BOL | 68 |

## Bosnia & Herzegovina

| Sarajevo | 387 | Convertible Mark | BAM |
|----------|-----|------------------|-----|
| +1 | BA | BIH | 70 |

## Botswana

| Gaborone | 267 | Pula | BWP |
|----------|-----|------|-----|
| +2 | BW | BWA | 72 |

## Brazil

| Brasilia | 55 | Real | BRL |
|----------|-----|------|-----|
| -3 | BR | BRA | 76 |

## Brunei

| Bandar Seri Begawan | 673 | Brunei Dollar | BND |
|---------------------|-----|---------------|-----|
| +8 | BN | BRN | 96 |

## Bulgaria

| Sofia | 359 | Lev | BGL |
|-------|-----|-----|-----|
| +2 | BG | BGR | 100 |

## Burundi

| Bujumbura | 257 | Burundi Franc | BIF |
|-----------|-----|---------------|-----|
| +2 | BI | BDI | 108 |

## Cambodia

| Phnom Penh | 855 | Riel | KHR |
|------------|-----|------|-----|
| +7 | KH | HKM | 116 |

## Cameroon

| Yaounde | 267 | CFA Franc BEAC | XAF |
|---------|-----|----------------|-----|
| +1 | CM | CMR | 120 |

## Canada

| Ottawa | 1 | Canadian Dollar | CAD |
|--------|---|-----------------|-----|
| -5 | CA | CAN | 124 |

## Central African Republic

| Bangui | 236 | CFA Franc BEAC | |
|--------|-----|----------------|---|
| +1 | CF | CAF | 140 |

## Chad

| N'Djamena | 235 | CFA Franc BEAC | XAF |
|-----------|-----|----------------|-----|
| +1 | TD | TCD | 148 |

## Chile

| Santiago | 56 | Chilean Peso | CLP |
|----------|-----|--------------|-----|
| -4 | CL | CHL | 152 |

## China, People's Republic of

| Beijing | 86 | Renminbi Yuan | CNY |
|---------|-----|---------------|-----|
| +8 | CN | CHN | 156 |

## Colombia

| Bogota | 57 | Colombian Peso | COP |
|--------|-----|----------------|-----|
| -5 | CO | COL | 170 |

## Congo, Democratic Republic of (Zaire)

| Kinshasa | 243 | New Zaire | ZRN |
|----------|-----|-----------|-----|
| +1 | CD | COD | 180 |

## Congo

| Brazzaville | 242 | CFA Franc BEAC | XOF |
|-------------|-----|----------------|-----|
| +1 | CG | COG | 178 |

## Costa Rica

| San Jose | 506 | Costa Rican Colon | CRC |
|----------|-----|-------------------|-----|
| -6 | CR | CRI | 188 |

## Croatia

| Zagreb | 385 | Kuna | HRK |
|--------|-----|------|-----|
| +1 | HR | HRV | 191 |

## Cuba

| Havanna | 53 | Cuban Peso | CUP |
|---------|-----|------------|-----|
| -5 | CU | CUB | 192 |

## Czech Republic

| Prague | 420 | Czech Koruna | CZK |
|--------|-----|--------------|-----|
| +1 | CZ | CZE | 203 |

## Denmark

| Copenhagen | 45 | Danish Krone | DKK |
|------------|-----|--------------|-----|
| +1 | DK | DNK | 208 |

## Dominican Republic

| Santo Domingo | 1 | Dominican Republic Peso | DOP |
|---------------|-----|-------------------------|-----|
| -4 | DO | DOM | 214 |

## Ecuador

| Quito | 593 | US Dollar | USD |
|-------|-----|-----------|-----|
| -5 | EC | ECU | 218 |

## Egypt

| Cairo | 20 | Egyptain Pound | EGP |
|-------|-----|----------------|-----|
| +2 | EG | EGY | 818 |

## El Salvador

| San Salvador | 503 | El Salvadorian Colon | SVC |
|--------------|-----|----------------------|-----|
| -6 | SV | SLV | 222 |

## Estonia

| Tallinn | 372 | Estonia Kroon | EEK |
|---------|-----|---------------|-----|
| +2 | EE | EST | 233 |

## Ethiopia

| Assis Ababa | 251 | Birr | ETB |
|---|---|---|---|
| +3 | ET | ETH | 231 |

## Finland

| Helsinki | 358 | Euro | EUR |
|---|---|---|---|
| +2 | FI | FIN | 246 |

## France

| Paris | 33 | Euro | EUR |
|---|---|---|---|
| +1 | FR | FRA | 250 |

## French Guiana

| Cayenne | 594 | Euro | EUR |
|---|---|---|---|
| -3 | GF | GUF | 254 |

## Gabon

| Libreville | 241 | CFA Franc BEAC | XAF |
|---|---|---|---|
| +1 | GA | GAB | 266 |

## Gambia, The

| Banjul | 220 | Dalasi | GMD |
|---|---|---|---|
| 0 | GM | GMB | 270 |

## Georgia

| Tbilisi | 995 | Lari | GEL |
|---|---|---|---|
| +3 | GE | GEO | 268 |

## Germany

| Berlin | 49 | Euro | EUR |
|---|---|---|---|
| +1 | DE | DEU | 276 |

## Ghana

| Accra | 233 | Cedi | GHC |
|-------|-----|------|-----|
| 0     | GH  | GHA  | 288 |

## Greece

| Athens | 30 | Euro | EUR |
|--------|-----|------|-----|
| +2     | GR  | GRC  | 300 |

## Guatemala

| Guatemala City | 502 | Quetzal | GTQ |
|----------------|-----|---------|-----|
| -6             | GT  | GTM     | 320 |

## Guinea

| Conakry | 224 | Guinea Franc | GNF |
|---------|-----|--------------|-----|
| 0       | GN  | GIN          | 324 |

## Guyana

| Georgetown | 592 | Guyana Dollar | GYD |
|------------|-----|---------------|-----|
| -3         | GY  | GUY           | 328 |

## Haiti

| Port-au-Prince | 509 | Gourde | HTG |
|----------------|-----|--------|-----|
| -5             | HT  | HTI    | 332 |

## Honduras

| Tegucigalpa | 504 | Lempira | HNL |
|-------------|-----|---------|-----|
| -5          | HN  | HND     | 340 |

## Hong Kong

| Hong Kong | 852 | Hong Kong Dollar | HKD |
|-----------|-----|------------------|-----|
| +8        | HK  | HKG              | 344 |

## Hungary

| Budapest | 36 | Forint | HUF |
|---|---|---|---|
| +1 | HU | HUN | 348 |

## Iceland

| Reykjavik | 354 | Krona | ISK |
|---|---|---|---|
| 0 | IS | ISL | 352 |

## India

| New Delhi | 91 | Rupee | INR |
|---|---|---|---|
| +5 1/2 | IN | IND | 356 |

## Indonesia

| Jakarta | 62 | Rupiah | IDR |
|---|---|---|---|
| +7 | ID | IDN | 360 |

## Iran

| Tehran | 98 | Rial | IRR |
|---|---|---|---|
| +4 | IR | IRN | 364 |

## Iraq

| Baghdad | 964 | Iraqi Dinar | IQD |
|---|---|---|---|
| +3 | IQ | IRQ | 368 |

## Ireland

| Dublin | 353 | Euro | EUR |
|---|---|---|---|
| 0 | IE | IRL | 372 |

## Israel

| Jerusalem | 972 | New Shekel | ILS |
|---|---|---|---|
| +2 | IL | ISR | 376 |

## Italy

| Rome | 39 | Euro | EUR |
|------|------|------|------|
| +1 | IT | ITA | 380 |

## Ivory Coast

| Yamoussoukro | 225 | CFA Franc BCEAO | XOF |
|------|------|------|------|
| 0 | CI | CIV | 384 |

## Jamaica

| Kingston | 1 | Jamaican Dollar | JMD |
|------|------|------|------|
| -5 | JM | JAM | 388 |

## Japan

| Tokyo | 81 | Yen | JPY |
|------|------|------|------|
| +9 | JP | JPN | 392 |

## Jordan

| Amman | 962 | Jordanian Dinar | JOD |
|------|------|------|------|
| +3 | JO | JOR | 400 |

## Kazakhstan

| Almaty | 7 | Tenge | KZT |
|------|------|------|------|
| +6 | KZ | KAZ | 398 |

## Kenya

| Nairobi | 254 | Kenyan Shilling | KES |
|------|------|------|------|
| +3 | KE | KEN | 404 |

## Korea, North

| Pyongyang | 850 | North Korean Won | KPW |
|------|------|------|------|
| +9 | KP | PRK | 408 |

## Korea, South

| Seoul | 82 | South Korean Won | KRW |
|-------|-----|------------------|-----|
| +9 | KR | KOR | 410 |

## Kuwait

| Kuwait | 965 | Kuwaiti Dinar | KWD |
|--------|-----|---------------|-----|
| +3 | KW | KWT | 414 |

## Kyrgyzstan

| Bishkek | 996 | Kyrgyzatan Som | KGS |
|---------|-----|----------------|-----|
| +5 | KG | KGZ | 417 |

## Laos

| Vientiane | 856 | Kip | LAK |
|-----------|-----|-----|-----|
| +7 | LA | LAO | 418 |

## Latvia

| Riga | 371 | Lat | LVL |
|------|-----|-----|-----|
| +2 | LV | LVA | 428 |

## Lebanon

| Beirut | 961 | Lebanese Pound | LBP |
|--------|-----|----------------|-----|
| +2 | LB | LBN | 422 |

## Lesotho

| Maseru | 266 | Loti | LSL |
|--------|-----|------|-----|
| +2 | LS | LSO | 426 |

## Liberia

| Monrovia | 231 | Liberian Dollar | LRD |
|----------|-----|-----------------|-----|
| 0 | LR | LBR | 430 |

## Libya

| Tripoli | 218 | Libyan Dinar | LYD |
|---------|-----|--------------|-----|
| +2      | LY  | LBY          | 434 |

## Lithuania

| Vilnius | 370 | Litas | LTL |
|---------|-----|-------|-----|
| +2      | LT  | LTU   | 440 |

## Luxembourg

| Luxembourg | 352 | Euro | EUR |
|------------|-----|------|-----|
| +1         | LU  | LUX  | 442 |

## Macedonia

| Macedonia | 389 | Denar | MKD |
|-----------|-----|-------|-----|
| +1        | MK  | MKD   | 807 |

## Madagascar

| Antananarivo | 261 | Malagasy Franc | MGF |
|--------------|-----|----------------|-----|
| +3           | MG  | MDG            | 450 |

## Malawi

| Lilongwe | 265 | Kwacha | MWK |
|----------|-----|--------|-----|
| +2       | MW  | MWI    | 454 |

## Malaysia

| Kuala Lumpur | 60 | Ringgit | MVR |
|--------------|----|---------|-----|
| +8           | MY | MYS     | 458 |

## Mali

| Bamako | 223 | CFA Franc BCEAO | XOF |
|--------|-----|-----------------|-----|
| 0      | ML  | MLI             | 466 |

## Mauritania

| Nouakchotte | 222 | Ouguiya | MRO |
|---|---|---|---|
| 0 | MR | MRT | 478 |

## Mauritius

| Port Louis | 230 | Mauritius Rupee | MUR |
|---|---|---|---|
| +4 | MU | MUS | 480 |

## Mexico

| Mexico City | 52 | Mexican Peso | MXN |
|---|---|---|---|
| -6 | MX | MEX | 484 |

## Moldova

| Kishinev | 373 | Leu | MDL |
|---|---|---|---|
| +2 | MD | MDA | 498 |

## Mongolia

| Ulan Bator | 976 | Tugrik | MNT |
|---|---|---|---|
| +8 | MN | MNG | 496 |

## Montenegro & Serbia

| Belgrade | 381 | Yugoslavian Dinar | YUM |
|---|---|---|---|
| +1 | YU | YUG | 891 |

## Morocco

| Rabat | 212 | Morrocan Dirham | MAD |
|---|---|---|---|
| 0 | MA | MAR | 504 |

## Mozambique

| Maputo | 258 | Metical | MZM |
|---|---|---|---|
| +2 | MZ | MOZ | 508 |

### Myanmar (Burma)

| Yangon | 95 | Kyat | **MMK** |
|--------|----|------|---------|
| +6 1/2 | MN | MMR | 104 |

### Namibia

| Windhoek | 264 | Namibian Dollar | **NAD** |
|----------|-----|-----------------|---------|
| +2 | NA | NAM | 516 |

### Nepal

| Kathmandu | 977 | Nepalese Rupee | **NPR** |
|-----------|-----|----------------|---------|
| +5 3/4 | NP | NPL | 524 |

### Netherlands

| Amsterdam | 31 | Euro | **EUR** |
|-----------|----|------|---------|
| +1 | NL | NLD | 528 |

### New Zealand

| Wellington | 64 | New Zealand Dollar | **NZD** |
|------------|----|--------------------|---------|
| +12 | NZ | NZL | 554 |

### Nicaragua

| Managua | 505 | Cordoba | **NIC** |
|---------|-----|---------|---------|
| -6 | NI | NIC | 558 |

### Niger Republic

| Niamey | 227 | CFA Franc BCEAO | **XOF** |
|--------|-----|-----------------|---------|
| +1 | NE | NER | 562 |

### Nigeria

| Abuja | 234 | Naira | **NGN** |
|-------|-----|-------|---------|
| +1 | NG | NGA | 566 |

## Norway

| Oslo | 47 | Norwegian Krone | NOK |
|------|-----|-----------------|-----|
| +1   | NO  | NOR             | 578 |

## Oman

| Muscat | 968 | Rial Omani | OMR |
|--------|-----|------------|-----|
| +4     | OM  | OMN        | 512 |

## Pakistan

| Islamabad | 92 | Pakistani Rupee | PKR |
|-----------|-----|-----------------|-----|
| +5        | PK  | PAK             | 586 |

## Panama

| Panama City | 507 | Balboa | PAB |
|-------------|-----|--------|-----|
| -5          | PA  | PAN    | 591 |

## Papua New Guinea

| Port Moresby | 675 | Kina | PGK |
|--------------|-----|------|-----|
| +10          | PG  | PNG  | 598 |

## Paraguay

| Asuncion | 595 | Guarani | PYG |
|----------|-----|---------|-----|
| -4       | PY  | PRY     | 600 |

## Peru

| Lima | 51 | New Sol | PEN |
|------|-----|---------|-----|
| -5   | PE  | PER     | 604 |

## Philippines

| Manila | 63 | Philippine Peso | PHP |
|--------|-----|-----------------|-----|
| +8     | PH  | PHL             | 608 |

## Poland

| Warsaw | 48 | New Zloty | PLN |
|--------|----|-----------|-----|
| +1 | PL | POL | 616 |

## Portugal

| Lisbon | 351 | Euro | EUR |
|--------|-----|------|-----|
| 0 | PT | PRT | 620 |

## Romania

| Bucharest | 40 | Leu | ROL |
|-----------|----|-----|-----|
| +2 | RO | ROM | 642 |

## Russia

| Moscow | 7 | Ruble | RUB |
|--------|---|-------|-----|
| +3 | RU | RUS | 643 |

## Rwanda

| Kigali | 250 | Rwanda Franc | RWF |
|--------|-----|--------------|-----|
| +2 | RW | RWA | 646 |

## Saudi Arabia

| Riyadh | 966 | Saudi Riyal | SAR |
|--------|-----|-------------|-----|
| +3 | SA | STP | 682 |

## Senegal

| Dakar | 221 | CFA Franc BCEAO | XOF |
|-------|-----|-----------------|-----|
| 0 | SN | SEN | 686 |

## Sierra Leone

| Freetown | 232 | Leone | SLL |
|----------|-----|-------|-----|
| 0 | SL | SLE | 694 |

## Singapore

| Singapore | 65 | Singapore Dollar | SGD |
|-----------|-----|------------------|-----|
| +8 | SG | SGP | 702 |

## Slovak Republic

| Bratislava | 421 | Slovak Koruna | SKK |
|------------|-----|---------------|-----|
| +1 | SK | SVK | 703 |

## Slovenia

| Ljubljana | 386 | Tolar | SIT |
|-----------|-----|-------|-----|
| +1 | SI | SVN | 705 |

## Somalia

| Mogadishu | 252 | Somali Shilling | SOS |
|-----------|-----|-----------------|-----|
| +3 | SO | SOM | 706 |

## South Africa

| Cape Town | 27 | Rand | ZAR |
|-----------|-----|------|-----|
| +2 | ZA | ZAF | 710 |

## Spain

| Madrid | 34 | Euro | EUR |
|--------|-----|------|-----|
| +1 | ES | ESP | 724 |

## Sri Lanka

| Colombo | 94 | Sri Lankan Rupee | LKR |
|---------|-----|------------------|-----|
| +5 1/2 | LK | LKA | 144 |

## Sudan

| Khartoum | 249 | Sudanese Dinar | SDD |
|----------|-----|----------------|-----|
| +2 | SD | SDN | 736 |

## Suriname

| Paramaribo | 597 | Suriname Guilder (florin or gulden) | SRG |
|---|---|---|---|
| -3 | SR | SUR | 740 |

## Swaziland

| Mbabane | 268 | Lilangeni Emalangeni | SZL |
|---|---|---|---|
| +2 | SZ | SWZ | 478 |

## Sweden

| Stockholm | 46 | Swedish Krona | SEK |
|---|---|---|---|
| +1 | SE | SWE | 752 |

## Switzerland

| Bern | 41 | Swiss Franc | CHF |
|---|---|---|---|
| +1 | CH | CHE | 756 |

## Syria

| Damascus | 963 | Syrian Pound | SYP |
|---|---|---|---|
| +2 | SY | STR | 760 |

## Taiwan

| Taipei | 886 | Taiwan Dollar | TWD |
|---|---|---|---|
| +8 | TW | TWN | 158 |

## Tajikistan

| Dushanbe | 992 | Tajikistan Ruble Somoni | TJR TJS |
|---|---|---|---|
| +5 | TJ | TJK | 762 |

## Tanzania

| Dar es Salaam | 255 | Tanzanian Shilling | TZS |
|---|---|---|---|
| +3 | TZ | TZA | 843 |

## Thailand

| Bangkok | 66 | Baht | THB |
|---|---|---|---|
| +7 | TH | THA | 764 |

## Tunisia

| Tunis | 216 | Tunisian Dinar | TND |
|---|---|---|---|
| +1 | TN | TUN | 788 |

## Turkey

| Ankara | 90 | Turkish Lira | TRL |
|---|---|---|---|
| +2 | TR | TUR | 792 |

## Turkmenistan

| Ashgabat | 993 | Manat | TMM |
|---|---|---|---|
| +5 | TM | TKM | 795 |

## Uganda

| Kampala | 256 | Ugandian Shilling | UDX |
|---|---|---|---|
| +3 | UG | UGA | 800 |

## Ukraine

| Kiev | 380 | Hryvan | UAH |
|---|---|---|---|
| +2 | UA | UKR | 804 |

## United Arab Emirates

| Abu Dhabi | 971 | UAE Dirham | AED |
|---|---|---|---|
| +4 | AE | ARE | 784 |

## United Kingdom

| London | 44 | Pound Sterling | GBP |
|--------|-----|----------------|-----|
| 0 | GB | GBR | 826 |

## United States

| Washington | 1 | US Dollar | USD |
|------------|---|-----------|-----|
| -5 | US | USA | 840 |

## Uruguay

| Montevideo | 598 | Uruguayan New Peso | UYN |
|------------|-----|--------------------|-----|
| -3 | UY | URY | 858 |

## Uzbekistan

| Tashkent | 998 | Uzbek Som | UZS |
|----------|-----|-----------|-----|
| +5 | UZ | UZB | 860 |

## Venezuela

| Caracas | 58 | Venezuela Bolivar | VEB |
|---------|-----|-------------------|-----|
| -4 | VE | VEN | 862 |

## Vietnam

| Hanoi | 84 | New Dong | VND |
|-------|-----|----------|-----|
| +7 | VN | VNM | 704 |

## Zambia

| Lusaka | 260 | Kwacha | ZMK |
|--------|-----|--------|-----|
| +2 | ZM | ZMB | 894 |

## Zimbabwe

| Harare | 263 | Zimbabwe Dollar | ZWD |
|--------|-----|-----------------|-----|
| +2 | ZW | ZWE | 716 |

# *Glossary*

**Air Waybill (AWB)**  A bill of lading used for air transportation. An air waybill outlines the terms of agreement between the carrier and shipper for transporting the goods and contain limitations of liability. Also known as an airbill.

**Bill of Lading**  A negotiable or non-negotiable contract issued by a carrier (mostly rail, ocean, and truck carriers) which serves as receipt for the goods to be delivered to a designated person. This document sets out the conditions of a contract between the shipper and the carrier.

**Bonded Warehouse** A facility in which goods subject to taxes or customs duties are temporarily stored without the payment of taxes. A bond or security is given for the payment of all taxes and duties that would be payable if the goods were imported. Operations in the warehouse might include such things as assembly, manipulation, packaging, or storage.

**Brokerage Fees** Fees charged by a customs broker for preparing the release information and accounting for goods required by customs in the country of import. Also known as Entry Preparation Charge or Customs Clearance Fee.

**Carrier** A legal entity that is in the business of transporting passengers or goods for hire.

**CFR (Cost and Freight)** See Incoterms in Chapter 21.

**Commercial Goods** Goods imported into a country for sale or for any commercial, industrial, occupational, institutional, or other similar use.

**Consolidation** The practice of combining multiple small shipments into one larger order to lower freight and customs clearance costs.

**Container** A reusable, rigid, exterior box for shipping merchandise by air, vessel, truck, or rail.

**CIF (Cost, Insurance and Freight)** See Incoterms in Chapter 21.

**Country of Origin** The country in which goods were produced, mined, grown, or manufactured.

**Customs** The government service which is responsible for the administration of customs law and the collection of duties and taxes relating thereto and which has responsibility for the application of other laws and regulations relative to the importation, transit, and exportation of goods.

**Customs Broker** A person or company in the country of import that is licensed by that country's government to act as an agent on behalf of the importer to transact business relating to importing or exporting goods. Some customs brokers also act as freight forwarders.

**Customs Duties** Import taxes imposed on imported goods by customs in the importing country at rates specified in that country's tariff.

**Customs Offices** A place designated by the country into which the goods are being imported that includes the place where goods are DDP (Delivered Duty Paid). See Incoterms in Chapter 21.

**Customs-Trade Partnership Against Terrorism (C-TPAT)** A joint US-Canada government initiative to strengthen border security.

**DDU (Delivered Duty Unpaid)** See Incoterms in Chapter 21.

**Declared Value For Carriage** The value of goods declared to the carrier for the purposes of determining charges and establishing the liability of the carrier. See Incoterms in Chapter 21.

**Declared Value for Customs** The value of a shipment according to the customs laws of the destination country required to be declared on the shipping documents or by the importer when he presents the goods for customs clearance.

**Distribution Service** A transportation service that accepts a shipment from a shipper and at a destination location that separates and sorts the packages and distributes them to many receivers.

**Distributor** An agent who sells for a supplier at wholesale and usually maintains an inventory of the supplier's products.

**Door-To-Door Shipping** Service from shippers door to consignee's door.

**Drawback** A claim to the government for the refund of import duties and taxes, in whole or in part, when the imported goods are re-exported in the same condition or used in the manufacture of exported goods.

**Duty**  The import tax imposed by customs on imported goods.

**Duty Free**  Goods that are not subject to duty under the customs tariff.

**Entry**  The formal process by which goods are imported into a country consisting of filing of documents with the importing country's customs service and the payment of customs duties.

**Examination**  The inspection of goods or conveyances.

**Export License**  A government document issued by the exporting country that allows the licensee to export designated controlled goods to specified destinations. This document is required to import the goods into the country of destination.

**Export Quotas**  Specified maximums which a country places on the value or volume of certain of its exports.

**EXW (Ex Works)**  See Incoterms in Chapter 21.

**FOB (Free On Board)**  See Incoterms in Chapter 21.

**Free and Secure Trade (FAST)**  A joint Canada-US initiative that offers harmonized commercial process to pre-approved importers, carriers, and registered drivers for transporting pre-approved eligible goods across the border quickly (e.g., for truck transportation).

**Free Zone**  An area within a country (a seaport, airport, warehouse, or any designated area) regarded as being outside its customs territory where importers may bring goods of foreign origin without paying customs duties and taxes, pending their eventual processing, transshipment, or re-exportation. Also referred to as a Foreign Trade Zone (FTZ).

**Freight Forwarder**  A company that forwards shipments via common carriers, arranges space for those shipments on behalf of exporters, and processes the documentation or performs related activities to those shipments. Some freight forwarders also act as customs brokers.

**Harmonized System (HS)**  The tariff system is an international goods classification system developed by the World Customs Organization (includes most of the trading nations in the world) for classifying imported and exported products. Common international classifications facilitate balance of trade statistics collection, customs classification, and country of origin determination. The first six digits of the HS number classify the goods internationally and the remaining 2 or 4 digits (depending on the country of import) provide information for duty assessment and statistical information.

**High Value Shipments (HVS)**  Identifies an import shipment entering Canada valued at over $1,600 (Canadian Dollars).

**Importer**  A person or company responsible to arrange for presentation of the proper accounting documents for imported goods and paying the related duties and taxes owed.

**Import Quota**  A protective device establishing limits on the quantity of a particular product that may be imported into a country.

**In Bond**  Subject to customs control in the country of import, goods can enter in bond to an inland customs office or bonded warehouse.

**Incoterms 2000**  A standard set of trading terms and definitions most commonly used in international sales contracts. First published in 1936 by the International Chamber of Commerce they are accepted by governments and legal authorities worldwide. See Incoterms in Chapter 21.

**Informal Entry**  A simplified import entry procedure accepted at the option of US Customs for any baggage or commercial shipment that does not exceed a specified value.

**In Transit**  The movement of goods through a country's territory from a point outside that country to another foreign point.

**Less than Container Load (LCL)** Goods transported by ocean that are less than a full container.

**Less than Truckload (LTL)** Most goods transported over the road by common carrier are referred to as LTL shipments. Less than a full truckload.

**Letter of Credit (LC)** A commitment, usually by a bank on behalf of a client (buyer), to pay a beneficiary (seller) a stated amount of money under specified conditions.

**Marking, Country of Origin** The physical markings on a product that indicate the country of origin where the article was produced.

**Merchandise Processing Fee (MPF)** A user-fee on imports levied by the US on goods imported into the country. The fees are collected at time of import. The fee does not apply to goods that qualify under NAFTA.

**Multi Modal** The practice of using more than one type of transportation (truck, rail, ocean, etc.) to deliver a shipment.

**Non-Resident Importer (NRI)** Term used for a shipper or exporter from another country who prepays all charges into Canada, including duties and taxes, and clears the goods into Canada in their name.

**North American Free Trade Agreement (NAFTA)** A free trade agreement signed between the United States, Canada, and Mexico implemented on January 1, 1994. Qualifying goods are duty free. In order for an importer to claim the duty free status under NAFTA, the exporter of the goods must provide a NAFTA Certificate of Origin. Goods must qualify under the NAFTA Rules of Origin.

**Ocean Bill of Lading (OBL)** A receipt for the cargo and a contract for transportation issued by an ocean carrier. When issued in negotiable form, it is also an instrument of title.

**Other Government Departments (OGDs)** Term used to refer to agencies and government departments other than the Canada Customs or the US Customs Service that impose import restrictions or documentation requirements. Customs in both countries administer these regulations at the time of importation.

**Port of Entry** A place designated for the formal entry and payment of duties to customs mainly located at sea ports, airports or land border crossings.

**Power of Attorney (POA)** Signed authorization given to a customs broker by the importer of the goods to act on behalf of the importer with customs. In Canada it is also referred to as a General Agency Agreement (GAA).

**Pre-Arrival Processing System (PAPS)** US Customs program that allows approved driver to forward shipment information to the border in advance of arrival to expedite the release of the shipment.

**Pre-Arrival Release System (PARS)** Canada Customs release system used to provisionally release goods prior to their arrival in Canada for shipments arriving through surface transport.

**Proof of Delivery** Information provided to the shipper by the carrier proving delivery of goods to the destination by signature, date, and time.

**Shippers Export Declaration (SED)** A form required by the US Treasury Department for shipments valued over $2,500 US ($500 US for mail shipments) for exports to all countries with the exception of Canada (it is required for a few selected Canadian goods). It is completed by the freight forwarder. The form is filed prior to physical export of the goods either by the seller of the goods or its forwarder. It is used for US export control and to provide trade statistics.

**Tariff** For a particular country, a comprehensive list of goods together with the duty (import tax) levied upon each.

**Temporary Importation** Goods imported under authorization for a limited period of time and specified use and for which total duties and taxes are not collected. The goods must be exported under customs supervision with the prescribed time frame or the full amount of duties and taxes must be paid.

**Transaction Value** The price actually paid for goods sold for export to another country to a purchaser in that country.

**Trans-Shipment** Movement of goods through one country to their ultimate destination.

**Valuation** Determination of the value of imported goods for the purpose of calculating the customs duty. The transaction value method is the primary method used for determining value. This method bases the value for duty upon the price paid, with certain adjustments, for goods sold for export to a purchaser in a foreign country.

**Value Added Tax (VAT)** An indirect tax on consumption that is levied at each discrete point in the chain of production and distribution, from the raw material to final consumption. Each processor or merchant pays a tax proportional to the amount by which he increases the value or marks up the goods he purchases for resale.

**World Customs Organization (WCO)** This organization is a co-operative council of customs organizations of the majority of countries worldwide. Its primary purpose is to facilitate the development of international trade through the improvement and harmonization of customs procedures. (*http://www.wco.net*)

**World Trade Organization (WTO)** The World Trade Organization replaced the General Agreement on Tariffs and Trade (GATT) on January 1, 1995. The GATT was founded on January 1, 1948, to reduce tariffs and other barriers to trade. Membership in the WTO now includes most trading nations around the world.

# *Bibliography*

This bibliography is to help you start building your trade reference system outlined in Chapter 4. We have selected and reviewed all the books listed out of a larger number. See other information resources in the appendices.

*A Basic Guide to Exporting* Third Edition, US Department of Commerce, Alexandra Woznick, World Trade Press, Novato, California, 1996, $20 US. A solid basic book on exporting with good references to other information.

*A Basic Guide to Importing* Third Editon, US Customs Service, NTC Business Books, Chicago, 1995, $10 US. A bare-bones but useful book on importing. A 1998 version of this book is on the Web at *http://www.unzco.com/basicguide* published by UNZ&CO.

*Dictionary of International Trade* Fifth Edition, Handbook of the Global Trade Community, Edward G. Hinkelman, World Trade Press, Novato, California, 2002, $45 US. A valuable reference for the import-export business.

*The Do's and Taboo's of International Trade* Revised Edition, A Small Business Primer, Roger E. Axtell, John Wiley & Sons, New York, 1994, $17 US. A basic book on import-export that goes beyond the procedural aspects and covers some of the cultural aspects.

*eBay the Smart Way* Third Edition, Joseph T. Sinclair, AMACOM, New York, 2004, $18 US. A basic book on using eBay to buy and sell.

*eBay Business the Smart Way*, Joseph T. Sinclair, AMACOM, New York, 2003, $25 US. A basic book on starting and running a business selling on eBay.

*Export/Import* Fourth Edition, Procedures and Documentation, Thomas E. Johnson, AMACOM, New York, 2002, $85. A comprehensive book providing much detail for those who desire to take a hands-on approach to the import-export business.

*Export Import* Third Edition, Joseph A. Zodl, Betterway Books, Cincinnati, 2002, $22 US. An easy-to-read basic book on import-export.

*Exporting Business*, Start and Run a Profitable Exporting Business, Laurel J. Delaney, Self-Counsel Press, Bellingham, Washington, 1998, $14 US. A solid basic book on exporting.

*Importers Manual* Fourth Edition, Edward G. Hinkelman, et al,

World Trade Press, Novato, California, $109 US. A comprehensive single-source reference for importers.

*Importing into the United States: A Guide for Commercial Importers*, US Customs, Books for Business, 2002, $13 US. A basic book on importing.

*International Payments, Letters of Credit, Documentary Collections and Cyberpayments in International Transactions*, Edward G. Hinkelman, World Trade Press, Novato, California, 1999, $20 US. An advanced book for those engaged in bulk imports and exports.

Variety of global trade books, World Trade Press, Novato, California, *http://worldtradepress.com*. World Trade Press does a great job of covering all aspects of international trade and offers a wide spectrum of useful books.

Although *eBay Global the Smart Way* provides a wealth of Web links to free information, it's always useful to have a few books at hand, too, that will make your day go smoother as you import or export as part of your eBay activities.

# Index

Λ&Λ Contract Customs Brokers, 33, 66
abbreviations, 47
accounting, 125
ACE USA, 184
addresses, confirmed, 131–132, 142, 143
administration, 124
Administrative Monetary Penalty System (AMPS), 24
advance payments, 98–99
advertising, *see* auction ads
agents, export, 216, *see also* freight forwarders
agricultural produce, 39, 50
air, goods arriving by, 43

Airborne Express, 163
air freight, 175
air waybill (AWB), 281
alcoholic beverages, 55, 57, 70, 72
AMPS (Administrative Monetary Penalty System), 24
anchovies, 72
animal feed, 72
animals, 70
Applied Language Solutions, 200
appraisals, customs, 88–89
arms, *see* weapons
attorneys general, state, 27
auction ads, 53, 170, 197

Australia, 149
Australian Dollars, 152
Austria, 149, 151
avionics devices, 56
AWB (air waybill), 281

Babel Fish (software), 16, 199, 202–205
bank fees, 123
banks
    currency exchange at, 118–119
    import-export, 24
    and letters of credit, 104–107
    loans from, 115–116
    PayPal accounts with, 139

banks (continued)
  visits to, 100
Bechtel, 244
Berlitz, 209–210
BidPay.com, 99
bill of lading number, 282
bills of lading, 107, 281
  ocean, 287
  through, 289
biological materials, 71
black listing, 165
boats, 71
bonded warehousing, 124, 237–238, 282
BookCenter.com, 224
bookmarks, browser, 31–32
brand names, 47
brokerage fees, 282
brokering, 246
brokers, *see* customs brokers
browser bookmarks, 31–32
bulk imports and exports, 42
  foreign licensing requirements for, 58
  and letters of credit, 105
  packaging for shipping of, 172
  payment for, 94
  placement of customs documents on, 52
  trade reference system for, 34
bulk purchases, 26
bulk shipping, 173–180
  containers for, 174–176
  and Incoterms 2000, 176–180
  insurance for, 184
  items for, 173–174
bureaucracy, 7–8, 24
Bureau of Export Administration (BXA), 56
Bureau of Industry and Security, 56
business cards, 213

business checks, 98
business culture, 210–213
business databases, 30
butter, 72
buyer protection plans, 134, 141
buyer(s)
  consumer, 16
  and credit, 105
  customs invoice listing of, 48
  customs obligations of, 52–53
  and fraud, 133–134
  and letters of credit, 106
  and payment, 96–98
  retail, 18
  as term, 177
buy options, 117
BuyUSA.com, 224
BXA (Bureau of Export Administration), 56

calendars, national, 208
call options, 117–118
cameras, 132
Canada, 6–7, 24
  classifications for, 88
  confirmed addresses for, 132
  cross-border warehousing in, 237, 240
  and customs brokers/freight forwarders, 64
  customs clearance fees in, 169
  customs invoices in, 47
  customs rulings for, 89
  duty-free maximum in, 42
  excise taxes in, 83
  export information for, 57, 73
  import restrictions in, 72
  minimum exemptions for duties in, 86
  and NAFTA, 48–50, 86–87
  as PayPal member country, 149

  ports of entry in, 42
  post offices in, 65
  rules and regulations information for, 73
  sales taxes in, 78–82
Canada Border Services Agency (CBSA), 73
Canada Post, 67, 167–170, 183
Canadian Dollars (CAD), 151
Canadian International Freight Forwarders Association (CIFFA), 65
Canadian Society of Customs Brokers, 65
cargo container transportation, 176
Carriage and Insurance Paid To (CIP), 178
Carriage Paid To (CPT), 178
carrier, 282
cashier's checks, 26, 99, 100, 148
Cash on Delivery (COD), 109
cash payments, 98
catalog sellers, 78–80
CBSA (Canada Border Services Agency), 73
certificate of origin, 49–50
CFR, *see* Cost and Freight
chambers of commerce abroad, 215
charge-backs, 98, 133, 134, 142
checks
  cashier's, 148
  letters of credit vs., 105–106
  personal/business, 98, 148
chemicals, 56
CIF (Cost, Insurance and Freight), 180
CIFFA (Canadian International Freight Forwarders Association), 65

CIP (Carriage and Insurance Paid To), 178
civil suits, 27
classification
    and duties, 88–89
    for licenses, 56
    product description for, 47
clearance, *see* customs clearance
closeouts, foreign, 19
clothing, 40, 57–58, 74
COD (Cash on Delivery), 109
collaboration software, 244–245
commercial goods, 282
commercial invoices
    as customs documents, 46–49
    for Indian customs, 166
    for letters of credit, 107
commodity groups, 88
common markets, 87
communication, 189–206
companies, joint ventures with, 223
compliance, 23–25, 167, 247–248
computers
    and cross-border warehousing, 240
    licenses required for exporting, 56, 57
    risk with sale of, 132
consignees, *see* buyers
consolidation, 282
consular offices (consulates)
    foreign, 51–52, 91
    and joint ventures, 225
    US, 214, 259
consumers
    eBay, 16–17
    tips for selling to foreign, 251–252
consumer sales, trade reference system for, 33–34
containers, 174–176, 282

contingency payments, 26, 104, 153–158
conversation, translators for, 200–201
copyrighted materials, 71, 249–250
cosmetics, 71
Cost, Insurance and Freight (CIF), 180
Cost and Freight (CFR), 179–180
costs, operational, *see* operational cost(s)
cotton, 72
counterfeit items, 71
*Country Business Guide,* 211
country of origin, 282
    and NAFTA, 48, 49, 87
    quotas issued in, 57
country profiles, 164–165
couriers (courier services)
    and customs documents, 52
    as freight forwarders, 66
    as information sources, 32
    insurance with, 182–183
    package shipping by, 162–168
    and packaging requirements, 123
    and retail buyers, 18
    subcontractors for, 97
    tracking systems of, 95
CPT (Carriage Paid To), 178
crafts items, 232–233
cream, 71
credit, 26, 100, *see also* letters of credit
credit cards, 21, 98
    and foreign exchange, 149
    multiple, 132
    PayPal-funded, 138, 139
    stolen, 132–133
creditors, 27

credit reports, 27
cross-border relationships, 219–226
    joint ventures as, 220–225
    with US Consulate, 225
    value of services vs., 220
cross-border warehousing, 53, 64, 124, 237, 238, 240
C-TPAT (Customs-Trade Partnership Against Terrorism), 283
cultural differences, 210–213
currency, 96
currency(-ies), 97
    dollars vs. foreign, 117
    exchanging, 118–119
    fees for exchange of, 123
    fluctuations in, 111–118
    and hedging, 111–120, 117–118
    payment with foreign, 146–148
    and PayPal, 151–152
    restrictions on exchange of, 120
customer service
    and customs brokers, 67–68
    customs brokers for premium, 53
    and customs clearance, 53
    door-to-door delivery as, 53, 64, 67–68
customs, 282
    classification by, 89
    inspections by, 40
    and restricted products, 50
    *see also specific headings*
customs broker(s), 59–68, 283
    acting as your own, 65
    alternatives to, 66–67
    choosing a, 62
    classification of goods by, 88

customs broker (continued)
  and customer service, 67–68
  customs clearance, 42–44
  and customs documents, 46
  definition of, 60
  fees for, 122
  finding a, 65–66
  forms from, 52
  and freight forwarders, 61, 63
  and insurance, 184
  and paying duties, 90
  for premium customer service,
    53
  role of, 60
  services provided by, 62–64
  UPS, 167
customs clearance, 39–44
  and freight forwarders, 62
  paperwork for, 43–44
  and payment, 97
  through ports of entry, 40–42
  through postal service, 67
  USPS for, 169
  value and volume consider-
    ations in, 42–43
customs document(s), 45–54
  and buyer's obligation, 52–53
  certificate of origin as, 49–50
  commercial invoice as, 46–49
  and customs brokers, 46, 60,
    62, 110
  and freight forwarders, 110
  getting assistance with, 51–52
  importance of, 46
  obtaining forms and samples
    of, 52
  placement of, on package, 52
  Shipper's Export Declaration
    as, 50
  and your obligation, 52
customs duties, 283
customs invoices, 25, 52

customs offices, 283
Customs-Trade Partnership
  Against Terrorism (C-
  TPAT), 283

DAF (Delivered At Frontier),
  178
dairy products, 70
damaged goods, 95, 96
DDP (Delivered Duty Paid),
  179
DDU (Delivered Duty Unpaid),
  179
declared value for carriage, 283
declared value for customs, 283
Delivered At Frontier (DAF),
  178
Delivered Duty Paid (DDP),
  179
Delivered Duty Unpaid (DDU),
  179
Delivered Ex Quay (DEQ), 180
Delivered Ex Ship (DES), 180
delivery
  door-to-door fret-free, 53, 67–
    68
  and payment, 95
DEQ (Delivered Ex Quay), 180
DES (Delivered Ex Ship), 180
Destination Control Statement,
  166
DHL, 163–164, 171, see also
  package shipping
DialPad, 195
dictionaries, 198
Dictionary of International Trade
  (Hinkelman), 174–176, 262
digital content, selling, 248–250
digital translations, 198–199
disputes, 131
distribution service, 283
distributor, 283

documentary collection, 99,
  109–110
documents
  and customs brokers, 60, 62
  for customs clearance, 43–44
  FedEx samples of, 166
  fees for preparation of, 122
  and freight forwarders, 61
  for letters of credit, 107–110
  for package shipping, 172
dollars, see US Dollar
door-to-door delivery service, 53,
  64
door-to-door fret-free delivery,
  67–68
door-to-door shipping, 283
drafts, foreign, 99, 148
drawback, 284
drugs, 55, 57, 71
Dun & Bradstreet's Guide to
  Doing Business Around the
  World (Morrison et al.)
duty free, 284
duty-free maximums, 42
duty(-ies), 8–9, 284
  calculation of, 87–91
  and customs brokers/freight
    forwarders, 63–64
  effect of, on marketing, 91–92
  in foreign countries, 90–92
  minimum exemptions for, 86
  as operational costs, 122–123
  paying, 90, 101
  and product classifications,
    88–89
  product exemptions for, 87
  questions to ask about, 85–86
  trade treaty exemptions for,
    86–87
DVD players, 132

Earth Calendar, 208

*eBay Business the Smart Way,* 11, 18, 125, 201, 246
eBay consumers, 16–17
eBay feedback system, 95, 128–130
eBay France, 202–205
eBay import-export businesses, 18–20
eBay International Trading Discussion Board, 200
*eBay Motors the Smart Way,* 12
eBay retail businesses, 17–18
eBay(s)
 foreign, 253–254
 learning the basics of, 11–12
 packing guide on, 172
 tips for importing to sell on, 255–256
 Universal Currency Converter on, 152
*eBay the Smart Way,* 11, 171, 246
eBay time, 261
ECCN (Export Control Classification Number), 56
eConsumer, 134
Elance, 246–247
electronics, 40, 56, 132
email, 139–140, 190–192, 197
encryption software, 57, 140
English language, 3–4
entry, 284
escrow, 133–134, 155–156
Escrow.com, 133
Escrow Europa, 134
escrow fees, 123
escrow-letter-of-credit arrangements, 109
European Common Market, 81, 87, 151, 240
European Union, 87
Euros, 151
examination, 284

exchange rates, 96
excise taxes, 83, 122–123
Executive Planet, 212
exemptions, duty, 86
explosives, 70
Export Administration Regulations, 56
export agents, 216
*Export America* (US GPO), 51
Export Assistance Centers, 30, 51, 91
Export.com, 212
Export Control Classification Number (ECCN), 56
exported goods, 6–7
exporters, 19–20
exporting
 joint ventures for, 222–223
 tips for, 257–258
export license, 284
export quotas, 284
exports
 bulk, 34
 and freight forwarders, 61
 getting assistance with, 51–52
 and payment of expenses, 100–101
 restricted, 56–57, 73
export trading companies, 216
EXW, 177–178

FAQs (Frequently Asked Questions), 35
FAS (Free Alongside Ship), 179
FAST (Free and Secure Trade), 284
"favorites" (Web), 30
fax, 197
FBI, 27
FCA (Free Carrier), 178
Federal Express (FedEx), 66, 161, 163–166, 171, 172, 182

Federal Trade Commission, 27
FedEx Global Trade Manager, 91
FedEx Ship Manager, 165
feed, animal, 72
feedback, eBay, 95, 128–130
fees
 bank, 123
 brokerage, 282
 currency exchange, 118–119, 146–148
 for letters of credit, 109
 payment of, 101
 PayPal, 138
financial services, 100, 119
financing, 24, 26–27, 106–107
flammable fabrics, 71
FOB (Free On Board), 179
food, 70, 73
Food and Drug Administration, 69–70
forced labor, 71
Foreign Agriculture Service, 212
foreign closeouts, 19
foreign consulates, 51–52, 91
foreign countries
 duties in, 90–91
 with high risk for fraud, 130–131
 list of basic information on, 260–280
 PayPal in, 143
 products manufactured in, 71
 sales taxes in, 79–80
 value-added taxes in, 80–83
 *see also* travel abroad
foreign drafts, 99, 100, 148
foreign eBays, buying on, 253–254
foreign licenses, 58
Foreignword, 198

forms
  customs, 52
  from customs brokers, 60
France, 150, 151, 202–205
fraud, 10, 127–134
  and buyers, 133–134
  countries with high risk for,
      130–131
  and eBay feedback system,
      130
  PayPal rates of, 140–142
  precautions for avoiding, 131–
      134
  resources on, 134
  risk of, 26
  and sellers, 131–133
Fraud.org, 134
FraudWatch International, 134
Free Alongside Ship (FAS), 179
Free and Secure Trade (FAST),
      284
Free Carrier (FCA), 178
Free On Board (FOB), 179
Free Translation, 199
free zone, 284
freight forwarders (freight con-
      solidators), 59–68, 284
  acting as your own, 65
  alternatives to, 66–67
  choosing a, 62
  and customer service, 67–68
  customs brokers, 62–64
  and customs brokers, 61, 63
  definition of, 61
  fees for, 122
  finding a, 65–66
  and insurance, 183
  and paying duties, 90
  role of, 61
Freightgate, 65
freight prepaid, 285

Frequently Asked Questions
      (FAQs), 35
fret-free delivery service, 53, 67–
      68
From Language to Language,
      198
fruit, 70
fur, 71

GAA (General Agency Agree-
      ment), 285
General Agency Agreement
      (GAA), 285
Germany, 6, 150, 151
Global Advisor (UPS), 91, 168
Global Airmail (USPS), 168
Global Delivery Services
      (USPS), 168
Global Economy (USPS), 168
Global Edge website, 212
Global Express Guaranteed
      (USPS), 168
Global Express (USPS), 168
global payments, see interna-
      tional payments
Global Priority Mail (USPS),
      168
Global Refund, 83
Global Road Warrior, 211
Global Trade Manager (FedEx),
      164, 166
gold, 71
Goods and Services Tax (GST),
      78–81, 285
Google, 199
government regulations, 9
  compliance with, 23–25, 167,
      247–248
  and customs brokers, 60
  and freight forwarders, 61
GPB (Pounds Sterling), 151

GPO, see US Government Print-
      ing Office
ground transportation, 66
GST, see Goods and Services Tax

handshaking, 212–213
Harmonized Commodity
      Description and Coding
      System, 88
Harmonized System (HS), 88,
      285
Harmonized Tariff number, 49
Harmonized Tariff Schedule, 88,
      89
hazardous substances, 71
headsets, 196
hedging, 117–118
high value shipments (HVS),
      285
household appliances, 71
HS (Harmonized System), 88
HumanTran, 200
hundredweight pricing, 285
HVS (high value shipments),
      285

IAC (International Access
      Code), 192
IFCBA (International Federa-
      tion of Customs Brokers
      Associations), 65
Iloxx SafeTrade, 134
import duties, see duty(-ies)
importers, 18–19, 60, 284
import-export banking, 24
import-export businesses
  eBay, 18–20
  and letters of credit, 107
  traditional, 20–21
import-export financial services,
      119

import-export service companies, 220
importing, joint ventures for, 221–222
import quota, 285
imports
    bulk, 34, 42
    duty-free maximums for, 42
    and payment of expenses, 100–101
    restricted, 69–73
    using customs brokers for facilitating, 43
in bond, 286
Incoterms 2000, 176–180, 285
indemnity, letters of, 107
Indemnity Insurance of North America, 184
India, 48, 57, 150, 166
industry techniques, 141
industry trade shows, 209
informal entry, 285
information, value of accurate and up-to-date, 9
information security, 56
inspections, customs, 40, 54
insurance, 95–96, 97, 101, 181–185
    agreement and responsibility for, 185
    cost of, 124
    with couriers, 182–183
    and customs brokers, 184
    and freight forwarders, 183
    with international bulk shipping, 184
    and managing general agents, 184
    with post office, 183
    third-party, 183
InsureCargo, 184

intellectual property, selling, 248–250
International Access Code (IAC), 192
International Business Culture and Etiquette website, 212
International Chamber of Commerce, 176
International Federation of Customs Brokers Associations (IFCBA), 65
International Mail Manual (USPS), 169
international payments, 145–152
    by cashier's check, 148
    by check, 148
    by credit card, 149
    by foreign draft, 148
    by money order, 148
    by PayPal, 149–152
    and price in foreign currencies, 147–148
    and price in US Dollars, 146–147
    receiving, 146
International Rate Tables (USPS), 169
International Resource Center
    FedEx, 166
    USPS, 169
International Sales Tax Refund Corporation, 83
International Trade Canada, 57, 73
Internet, 193–194, 243
Internet Service Providers (ISPs), 196
in transit, 285
inventory, 18–20
investors, 114–115
invoices, see commercial invoices; customs invoices

ISPs (Internet Service Providers), 196

jetports, 40–41
jewelry, 132
jobbers, buying from, 216
Johannesburg, 193
joint venturers, 20, 94, 216
joint ventures, 220–223
    with companies, 223
    for exporting, 222–223
    finding partners for, 223–225
    for importing, 221–222
    partnerships vs., 220–221
    and US Consulate, 225

Kinkos, 171
Kiss, Bow, or Shake Hands (Morrison et al.), 211

labels, shipping, 52
labor, forced, 71
Language Automation, 198
language issues, 3–6, 8, 198–201, 209–210
language translators, 16, 198–200
lasers, 56
lawsuits, 27
LCL, see less than container load
LCs, see letters of credit
less than container load (LCL), 61, 286
less than truckload (LTL), 286
letters of credit (LCs), 26, 99, 100, 103–110, 285
    bank's role in, 104–107
    contingency payments vs., 153–155
    cost of, 107
    documents required for, 107–110

letters of credit (continued)
  escrow vs., 123
  flexibility provided by, 105–
    106
  as form of credit, 104–105
  funding for, 106–107
  online, 108–109, 158
  purpose of, 107
letters of indemnity, 107
libraries, 30
licenses, 55–58
  of customs brokers, 60
  export, 284
  for exporting, 56–57
  foreign, 58
  for importing, 57
  and quotas, 57–58
  and restricted goods, 58
liquidation (of duties), 90
livestock, 70
loans, 115–116
logins, PayPal, 140
loss, risk of, 27
low value shipments (LVS), 286
LTL (less than truckload), 286
luxury taxes, 83
LVS (low value shipments), 286

machine tools, 71
Mailboxes, Etc, 171
managing general agents, 184
manufacturers' representatives,
    216
manufacturing abroad, 229–234
  of craft items, 232–233
  and labor rates, 229–230
  manufacturing in the USA vs.,
    233
  preparation for, 230–231
  and template products, 231–
    232
  and VAT, 233

marine systems, 56
markets, uniqueness of, 7
marking, country of origin, 286
maximums, duty-free, 42
meat, 70
merchandise processing fee
    (MPF), 286
Merchant Risk Council, 131
Mexico
  and NAFTA, 48–50, 86–87
  as PayPal member country,
    150
Michigan State University, 212
microorganisms, 56
milk, 71
minimum exemptions for duties,
    86
model numbers, 47
money, 71
Money Back Guarantee, 141
money orders, 99, 100, 148
motor vehicles, 71
MPF (merchandise processing
    fee), 287
MSNBC, 130
multi modal, 286

NAFTA, see North American
    Free Trade Agreement
NAFTA Certificate of Origin, 49
NAFTA statement, 49
narcotics, 71
National Customs Brokers &
    Forwarders Association of
    America (NCBFAA), 65
national security, 58
navigation devices, 56
NCBFAA (National Customs
    Brokers & Forwarders
    Association of America), 65
negotiations, 213
Net2phone, 195

neural network risk models, 141
Non-Resident Importers (NRIs),
    64, 237, 286
North American Free Trade
    Agreement (NAFTA), 48–
    50, 286
  and duties, 86–87
  rules of origin under, 48, 49,
    87
NRIs, see Non-Resident Import-
    ers
nuclear materials, 56
Numerica, 83
nuts, 70

obligations, customs
  buyer's, 52–53
  your, 52
OBL (ocean bill of lading), 286
ocean bill of lading (OBL), 286
off-eBay transactions, 128–129
OGGs, see Other Government
    Departments
olives, 72
Online Language Translators,
    200
online letters of credit, 108–109,
    158
online meetings, 244
operational cost(s), 121–125
  administration as, 124
  bank fees as, 123
  currency exchange fees as, 123
  customs broker/freight for-
    warder fees as, 122
  document preparation as, 122
  escrow fees as, 123
  insurance as, 124
  phone charges as, 124
  shipping as, 123–124
  special packaging as, 123
  taxes as, 122–123

operational cost (continued)
  trade reference system as, 122
  travel as, 124
  using accounting to manage, 125
  warehousing as, 124
origin, country of, 48
Other Government Departments (OGDs), 72, 286
package, attaching customs invoice to, 52
package shipping, 161–172
  avoiding damage when, 170–172
  by couriers, 162–168
  via post office, 168–170
packaging, special, 123
packaging services, 171
Packet 8, 195
paid coverage, 141
paperwork, 7–8
  and customs brokers, 60, 64
  for customs clearance, 43–44
  and freight forwarders, 64
  for letters of credit, 107–110
PAPS (Pre-Arrival Processing System), 288
PARS, see Pre-Arrival Release System
partners, 20, 94
partnerships, 220–222
Passport series (World Trade Press), 210–211
patent-pending methods, 141
payment(s), 8, 93–101
  advance, 98–99
  and buyer's concerns, 96–97
  contingency, 154–158
  contingent, 26
  by credit, 100
  and currency exchange factors, 111–120

and import/export expenses, 100–101
international, 145–152
letters of credit as promise of, 99, 103–110
PayPal, 138–140
and seller's concerns, 94–96
see also duty(-ies)
PayPal, 5, 20, 99, 137–144
  and confirmed addresses, 132
  and contingency payments, 156–158
  credit card- vs. bank-funded, 132–133
  currency exchange fees from, 123
  and escrow, 155–156
  exchange rates from, 151, 152
  in foreign countries, 143
  fraud rates with, 140–142
  getting help with, 143
  making payments via, 139, 140
  member countries of, 149–152
  receiving payments via, 138–140
  verification by, 129, 142–143
PayPal Help Center, 143
PayPal Security Center, 142
peanuts, 72
personal checks, 98, 148
pesticides, 71
petroleum products, 71
phone charges, 124
physical inspections, 54
Pickup on Demand, 169
plants, 70
POA, see power of attorney
pornography, 71
portals, 32–33
Port of Entry, 30
ports of entry, 40–42, 287

postage stamps, 71
Postal Inspector, 27
post office boxes, 131
post offices
  custom clearance by, 65
  as freight forwarders, 67
  insurance with, 183
  money orders from, 99
  as package shippers, 162
  package shipping via, 168–170
  and special packaging, 123
post-transaction screening, 140
poultry, 70
Pounds Sterling (GPB), 151
power of attorney (POA), 287
Pre-Arrival Processing System (PAPS), 287
Pre-Arrival Release System (PARS), 64, 287
Premier accountholders, 141
pre-transaction screening, 140
price
  in foreign currencies, 147–148
  in US Dollars, 146–147
price paid or payable, 288
pricing, hundredweight, 285
printed publications, 30–31
produce, 39
product exemptions, 87
product profit model, 125
profit, 114, 125
prohibited goods, 73
proof of delivery, 95, 132, 166, 287
proof of receipt, 95
propulsion systems, 56
provincial sales tax (PST), 79–81
Proz, 200
PST, see provincial sales tax
publications, 30–31
Purolator, 161, 167, 169
quotas, 57–58, 70

quotas (continued)
    and customs brokers, 60
    export, 284
    goods with, 71–72
    import, 285

radiation products, 70
radioactive materials, 70
radio frequency products, 70
Rand McNally, 211
receipt (of goods)
    proof of, 95
    undamaged, 96
records, keeping, 213
refunds, VAT, 82–83
relationships, cross-border, see
    cross-border relationships
Release on Minimum Docu-
    mentation (RMD), 288
restricted goods, 69–74
    clothing/electronics as, 40
    and customs brokers, 60
    customs documents for, 50
    for export, 56–57, 73
    for import, 58, 70–73
    list of, 70–71
    and minimum exemptions for
        duties, 86
    planning ahead when dealing
        in, 74
    rules and regulations concern-
        ing, 73
retail businesses, eBay, 17–18
revocability, 106
risk(s), 26–28
    with customs classifications,
        88–89
    with digital content, 250
    with foreign currency, 116
    fraud as, 127–134
    payment, 95, 97, 98

RMD (Release on Minimum
    Documentation), 288
rules of origin, 48, 49, 87

safety, 24, 26–28
St. Lawrence Seaway, 40, 41, 105
sales, consumer, 33–34
sales taxes, 77–84
    dealing with complexity of, 84
    excise taxes as, 83
    in foreign countries, 79–80
    as operational costs, 122–123
    in US, 78–79
    value-added taxes as, 80–83
Scambusters, 134
screening, transaction, 140
sea transportation, 179–180
Secure LC, 109, 158
security, national, 58
SED, see Shipper's Export Dec-
    laration
seeds, 70
self-classification, 88
self-insuring, 182
seller protection policy, 141
seller(s)
    consumer, 16–17
    and credit, 105
    customs invoice listing of, 48
    and fraud, 131–133
    and letters of credit, 106
    and payment, 94–96
    retail, 17–18
    as term, 177
sensors, 56
services, selling, 245–248
shaking hands, 212–213
ship, goods arriving by, 43
Shipper's Export Declaration
    (SED), 50, 287
shipping, 8
    cost of, 80, 82, 101, 123–124

and freight forwarders, 61
    see also specific headings
shipping agents, see freight for-
    warders
shipping labels, 52
shipping rates, 170
shopping abroad, 217
silver, 71
Skype, 195–196
small businesses, 154–155
small package service, 288
sole proprietorship, 114–115
space vehicles, 56
SquareTrade, 131
stamps, postage, 71
states
    attorneys general in, 27
    and sales taxes, 78
stolen credit cards, 132–133
Strategis, 73
sugar blends, 72
surface shipping, 123

tariff consulting, 167
tariffs, 49, 88, 89, 287
TAS (Trade Automation Ser-
    vice), 164
taxes, 8–9
    excise, 83, 122–123
    as operational costs, 122–123
    payment of, 101
    on sales, 77–84
    and travel deduction, 209, 217
    see also duty(-ies)
telecommunications, 56
telephone, 192–198
    calling abroad via, 192
    email vs., 197
telephone charges, 124
template products, 231–232
temporary importation, 287
terrorism, 54, 73

textiles, 57–58, 71, 72, 74
theft, risk of, 27
Thinking Voice service, 197–198
third-parties, 9
third-party insurance, 183
through bill of lading, 289
timeliness, 96, 113–114, 119
title, warranty of, 107
tourists, 83
toxic substances, 71
toxins, 56
tracking systems, 166
trade agreements, 70, 86–87
Trade Automation Service
    (TAS), 164
trade consulting, 167
trade deficit, 18–19
trademarked materials, 71
trade reference system, 29–35
    for bulk imports/exports, 34
    for classifications, 89
    for consumer sales, 33–34
    cost of, 122
    for duties, 91
    for excise taxes, 83
    FAQs for your, 35
    portals for your, 32–33
    publications for your, 30–31
    and sales taxes, 84
    websites in your, 31–32
TradeSecure, 133
trade shows, 209
transaction value, 288
translators
    consumer case study of, 201–
        205
    for conversation, 200–201
    digital, 198–199
    for writing, 199–200
transportation
    risks of, 27–28
    and safety, 24

travel abroad, 207–218
    buying during, 215–216
    costs of, 124
    and cultural differences, 210–
        213
    getting support during, 214–
        215
    and knowing the language,
        209–210
    and making contacts, 214–217
    making the most of, 213–214
    potential benefits of, 208–209
    preparing for, 209–210
    and shopping, 217
    tax deduction for, 209, 217
Triple Deal, 134
truck shipments, 64
tuna fish, 72

ULD (unit load devices), 175
United Parcel Service (UPS), 66,
    91, 100, 161, 163, 167–168,
    171, 182, 215
United States Council for Inter-
    national Business, 83, 92
unit load devices (ULD), 175
Universal Currency Converter,
    152
Universal Parcel Insurance Cov-
    erage, 183
UPS, see United Parcel Service
UPS Store, 171
UPS Trade Direct, 167
URL, 190
US Commercial Service offices,
    214
US Customs & Border Protec-
    tion, 42, 47, 70
    information on restricted
        products provided by,
        72, 73
    payment of duties to, 90

rulings by, 89
    website for, 73
US Department of Agriculture,
    39, 69, 212
US Department of Commerce,
    56, 91
US Department of Energy, 70
US Department of Homeland
    Security, 73
US Department of State, 51–52,
    259–260
US Dollar (USD), 112, 117,
    146–147, 151
US Government Printing Office
    (GPO), 51, 88
US Postal Service (USPS), 67,
    168–169, 182, 183

valuation, 288
value-added taxes (VAT), 80–83,
    288
    and manufacturing abroad,
        233
    as operational costs, 122–123
    refunds of, 81–82
value (of item), 47
VAT, see value-added taxes
Vatcollect, 83
vegetables, 70
verification, 129–130, 141–143
Verified Business accounthold-
    ers, 141
VeriTranslate, 200
video conferencing, 244
visas, 57
voice over IP (VoIP) services,
    195–196, 245
Vonage, 193–195, 245

warehousing, 235–241
    benefits of, 239–240
    bonded, 237–238, 282

warehousing (continued)
  costs of, 124
  cross-border, 53, 64, 237, 238
  by customs brokers/freight
      forwarders, 63–64
  in exporting country, 239
  and finding a warehouse, 240
  methods of, 236–238
warranty of title, 107
watch movements, 72
waybills, 52, 281
WCO, *see* World Customs Orga-
    nization
weapons, 55–57, 70
Wells Fargo Bank, 108–109
Western Union, 98, 99, 151, 152

whiskbrooms, 72
wire transfers, 26, 98, 100
Whitman, Meg, 247
wool, 71
WorldBiz.com, 212
World Customs Organization
    (WCO), 44, 53, 73, 88, 288
WorldLingo, 199
World Reference, 89
World Seller Program, 141
*World Trade Almanac,* 211
World Trade Centers, 215
World Trade Organization
    (WTO), 288
World Trade Press, 30, 32, 210–
    211

World Trade Reference portal,
    32–33, 211
written translations, 199–200
WTO (World Trade Organiza-
    tion), 290

Yen (JPY), 151